Bourdieu's Theory of the State

Steven Loyal

Bourdieu's Theory of the State

A Critical Introduction

Steven Loyal
School of Sociology
University College Dublin
Dublin, Ireland

ISBN 978-1-137-58349-9   ISBN 978-1-137-58350-5 (eBook)
DOI 10.1057/978-1-137-58350-5

Library of Congress Control Number: 2016957411

Cover illustration: Pattern adapted from an Indian cotton print produced in the 19th century

Printed on acid-free paper

This Palgrave Macmillan imprint is published by Springer Nature
The registered company is Nature America Inc.
The registered company address is: 1 New York Plaza, New York, NY 10004, U.S.A.

In a social world where the individual is increasingly becoming the sole focus, it is easy to forget that our actions presuppose and depend upon the material and emotional support of others. I'd like to dedicate this book to my family: my mother Lakhbir Kaur Loyal for her enduring, lifelong support; and to my partner, Andrea Berger who kindly tolerated and supported me during my unsocial work hours; and my son, Edgar Berger Loyal, who continues to suprise and fill me with a sense of wonder everyday

ACKNOWLEDGEMENTS

I would like to thank Andrew Linklater, Richard Kilminster, Jeremy Lane, Sinisa Malesevic and Steve Quilley for comments on various chapters of the book. I'd especially like to thank Bridget Fowler for going through the whole manuscript and making a number of insightful remarks and comments.

CONTENTS

CHAPTER 1

Introduction

Abstract This chapter looks at the difficulty of studying the state, introduces Pierre Bourdieu's theory of the state and sets out the plan of the book.

Keywords Bourdieu · State · State-formation · Symbolic power

Pierre Bourdieu is rightly regarded as one of the foremost modern sociologists of the modern era. In the English-speaking world his thought has traditionally been seen as passing from an early anthropological analysis of the uprooting of peasants in Algeria, to a sociology of practice, to an analysis of matrimonial strategies, domination and inequality in relation to education, art, culture, intellectuals, consumption, class and gender. This, of course, was partly an artefact of the haphazard translation of his work. Although the state began to play a more central role in much of his later thinking, Bourdieu never provided a unified theory of the state in his work, with the exception of a few articles and chapters in various books written in the mid- to late 1980s in France[1] and published in English

---

[1] Champagne, P., R. Remi-Lenoir, F. Poupeau, and M. C. Riviere. 'Position of the Lectures on the State in Pierre Bourdieu's Work' in Bourdieu, P. *On the State: Lectures at the Collège de France 1989–1991*. Edited by Patrick Champagne, Remi-Lenoir, Franck Poupeau and Marie-Christine Riviere. Cambridge: Polity, 2014, p. 379.

© The Author(s) 2017
S. Loyal, *Bourdieu's Theory of the State*,
DOI 10.1057/978-1-137-58350-5_1

1

from the 1990s.[2] As he noted in 1990: 'I only began to use the word "state" in my writing just two or three years ago. Up until then I never wrote "state", as I did not know what it was, but I did know enough to distrust the use of the concept, even as shorthand.'[3] His distrust of the concept stemmed from his sense that the idea of the state emerges from ordinary language and constitutes a 'pre-notion' – a socio-politically contested category that is an object rather than a tool for analysis. However, the recent publication of his lectures given over three academic years in the *Collège de France* between January 1990 and December 1991 in *On the State* goes some way to fill this gap.[4] This book demonstrates that the theory of the state plays a fundamental role in understanding his entire sociological *oeuvre*, especially with regard to the centrality accorded to the concepts of symbolic capital, symbolic power and symbolic violence; concepts he first systematically discussed in the mid-1970s.[5]

On the State is of great significance since it forces us to rethink and re-situate some of his other writings and ideas, especially the role of economic and cultural capital in social life as derivative and dependent upon symbolic capital and power. It then becomes possible to argue, as Wacquant has, that 'Bourdieu's entire *oeuvre* may be properly read as a quest to explicate the specificity and potency of symbolic power.'[6] Bourdieu's

---

[2] See Bourdieu, Pierre and Loic Wacquant. *An Invitation to Reflexive Sociology.* Cambridge: Polity Press, 1992; Bourdieu, Pierre. *The State Nobility: Elite Schools in the Field of Power.* Cambridge: Polity Press, 1998; Bourdieu, Pierre. 'Rethinking the State: Genesis and Structure of the Bureaucratic Field' in Bourdieu, Pierre. *Practical Reason: On the Theory of Action.* Cambridge: Polity Press, 1998, pp. 35–63; Bourdieu, Pierre. 'From the Kings House to the Reason of State: A Model of the Genesis of the Bureaucratic Field' in L. Wacquant (ed.) *Pierre Bourdieu and Democratic Politics: The Mystery of Ministry.* Cambridge: Polity, 2005.

[3] Bourdieu, Pierre. *On the State: Lectures at the Collège de France 1989–1992,* Edited by Patrick Champagne, Remi Lenoir, Franck Poupeau, and Marie-Christine Riviere, Cambridge: Polity Press, 2014, p. 113.

[4] Bourdieu, Pierre, *On the State.* Cambridge: Polity, 2014.

[5] See his essay 'On Symbolic Power' in Bourdieu, Pierre. *Language and Symbolic Power.* Cambridge: Polity, 1991, pp. 163–170; The concept of symbolic violence is also discussed in his book on schooling originally published in 1970, Bourdieu, Pierre and Jean-Claude Passeron. *Reproduction in Education, Society and Culture,* London: Sage, 1990.

[6] L. Wacquant (ed.) *Pierre Bourdieu and Democratic Politics: The Mystery of Ministry.* Cambridge: Polity 2005, p. 134.

analysis of the state, together with his discussion of the field of power, also allows us to understand in greater detail how social fields originate and are structured and shaped; an explanation that was heretofore missing from his work. It is the bureaucratic field, as part of the field of power, that controls other fields by regulating and legitimating them.

This book attempts to outline and critically reflect on Bourdieu's theory of the state partly by looking at it in relation to the secondary theories of the state he draws upon to develop his own theory of a specific state logic – the work of Marx, Weber, Durkheim, Elias, Tilly, and Corrigan and Sayer – and partly by contextualising it as a polemical intervention in the face of rising neo-liberalism.

In modern sociology, defining the nature of the state has always been a contested issue. The state remains recalcitrant to any tightly constructed conceptual or functional definition. As Bourdieu himself notes: 'The problem of the state is as complex as the problem of Being.'[7] This is not only because of the possibility, as Mann argues,[8] of defining states either in terms of their functions or the institutions they are composed of, or equally because the nature of states have changed over time – from city-states, to dynastic states, to nation-states – but also because modern states carry out a multiplicity of tasks in addition to their political function of governing and the production of legislation. Weber recognised this diversity in state functions when he noted that there were few activities that the state had not been involved in 'from the provision of subsistence to the patronage of the arts'.[9] More recently, Morgan and Orloff have referred to the state's ubiquitous and diverse presence in various social formations in terms of the 'many hands of the state'.[10] In his

---

[7] Bourdieu, Pierre. *On the State: Lectures at the College de France 1989–1992*, Edited by Patrick Champagne, Remi Lenoir, Franck Poupeau, and Marie-Christine Riviere. Cambridge: Polity Press, 2014, p. 30.

[8] Mann, Michael, 'The Autonomous Power of the State: Its Origins, Mechanisms, and Results' *Archives Europeens de sociology*, 25(4). 1984, p. 185.

[9] Weber, Max, Guenther Roth, Claus Wittich, and Claus Wittich. *Economy and Society: An Outline of Interpretive Sociology*. 2nd ed. Edited by Guenther Roth. Berkeley, CA: University of California Press, 1978, p. 58.

[10] Morgan, K. and A. Orloff. 'The Many Hands of the State' Buffet Series of International and Comparative Studies. Working Paper Series. No 14-001 December 2014.

'Notes on the Difficulty of Studying the State', Abrams argued that the concept of the state was 'one of those terms peculiarly apt to foster "an atmosphere of illusion" – a fallacy of confusion at best, an "official malefactor's screen" at worst, giving spurious concreteness and reality to that which has a merely abstract and formal existence'.[11] Both political sociologists and Marxists, he argued, had been trapped into a reified idea of the state as a substantial entity separate from society. Such a problematic understanding prevented social analysts from grasping the ideological nature of the state. Instead of studying the state as such, Abrams recommended the study of 'politically organized subjection'.[12]

Moreover, to add to these conceptual difficulties, sociological and political analyses of the state have tended to reflect the theorist's social, economic and political contexts albeit without being simply reducible to those contexts. Thus, it is difficult to understand Marx's writings on the state in France, Germany and Britain by divorcing them from the immediate context within which he was writing. This includes the political nature of his analysis designed to inform a revolutionary political practice – from his *Critique of Hegel's Theory of Law* (1975)[13] which takes the Prussian state as its background up to and including his remarks in *The Civil War in France* (1973)[14] which presupposes a centralised French state. Equally, Weber and Hintze's discussions of the state reflect the reality, policies and powers of the Prussian state extant in the late 19th and early 20th century, and although their work is less explicitly political, when compared to Marx and Engels, it is nevertheless also imbued with a determinate world-view shaping their understanding and explanation.

Understanding interpretations of the state partly as political interventions means that they need to be irreducibly situated in their social and political context. In the 1950s and 1960s pluralist perspectives that focused on states and governments in terms of their public policy decision-

---

[11] Abrams, Philip. 'Notes on the Difficulty of Studying the State' *Journal of Historical Sociology*, 1(1). 1988, p. 58.

[12] Ibid., p. 76.

[13] Marx, Karl. 1843. 'Contribution to a Critique of Hegel's Theory of Law' in L. Colletti (ed.) *Karl Marx: Early Writings*. London: Penguin, 1975.

[14] Marx, Karl. 1871. 'The Civil War in France' in D. Fernbach (ed.) *Karl Marx the First International and After*. Harmonsworth: Penguin, 1973.

making, and structural functionalism which examined the political sphere, rather than the state itself, emerged in the US within a liberal, democratic, capitalist state with dispersed domestic powers in the context of a post-war boom. A significant shift in perspective followed the student revolts of the late 1960s with the emergence of a number of Marxist analyses of the state, often under the influence of Althusser. This included the work of Nicos Poulantzas and Perry Anderson.[15] In the mid-1970s, with a burgeoning of Marxist theories of the state, the relation of the state to the capitalist economy led to a heated, though generally unproductive, dispute between Marxists such as Miliband[16] and Poulantzas.[17] The central question they posed of whether the state was a function of capitalist relations or a relatively autonomous entity was subsequently taken further by a Weberian approach that foregrounded the absolute autonomy of the state from economic and societal factors, especially in the work of Theda Skocpol and Michael Mann.[18]

The task of rethinking the state in light of Abrams' pioneering insights and analysing not only its economic and political functions but also its cultural and cognitive dimension was significantly carried forward by Corrigan and Sayer in their book *The Great Arch: State Formation as Cultural Revolution* (1985).[19] Their analyses in turn led to a growing

---

[15] Anderson, Perry. *Lineages of the Absolutist State*. London: Verso, 1974.

[16] Miliband, Ralph. 'The Capitalist State – Reply to Nicos Poulanzas' *New Left Review*, 59. 1970; Miliband, Ralph. *The State in Capitalist Society: The Analysis of the Western System of Power*. London: Quartet Books, 1973; Miliband, Ralph. 'Poulantzas and the Capitalist State' *New Left Review*, 82. 1973.

[17] Poulanzas, Nicos. 'The Problem of the Capitalist State' *New Left Review*, 58. 1969; Poulantzas, Nicos. 'The Capitalist State: A Reply to Miliband and Laclau' *New Left Review*, 95. 1976; Poulanzas, Nicos. *State, Power, Socialism*. London: New Left Books, 1978.

[18] Michael, Mann. *The Sources of Social Power: Volume 1, A History of Power from the Beginning to AD 1760: V. 1*. 1st ed. Cambridge, Cambridgeshire: Cambridge University Press, 1986; Mann, Michael. *The Sources of Social Power: Volume 2, the Rise of Classes and Nation-States, 1760–1914*. 2nd ed. United Kingdom: Cambridge University Press, 2012.

[19] Corrigan, Philip Richard D. and Derek Sayer. *The Great Arch: State Formation, Cultural Revolution and the Rise of Capitalism*. New York, NY: Blackwell Publishers, 1985.

body of work examining the cultural, ideational and symbolic aspects of the state. A central figure in this growing corpus was Bourdieu.[20]

Bourdieu's theory of the state, like much of his work in general, can be difficult to understand. *On the State* (2014), containing lectures given at the *Collège de France*, provides an important outline but is full of asides, detours and is repetitive as well as being intentionally recursive. This partly reflects the fact that these are lectures not necessarily intended for publication but also the fact that Bourdieu is himself grappling with the problem of defining the state as he tries to outline a sociological discourse about it.

This book aims to provide a more accessible version of his theory as well as situating it politically and intellectually. In Chapter 2, we discuss Bourdieu's general sociological approach, looking at his work as a worldview that incorporates five major phases of development as well as discussing some of his key concepts, including habitus, field, capital, reflexivity and symbolic power. In Chapter 3, we selectively review some theories of the state in relation to which Bourdieu's develops his own position. This includes the theories of Marx, Weber and Durkheim, but also the modern approaches to the state contained in the work of Elias, Tilly, and Corrigan and Sayer. In Chapter 4, we examine Bourdieu's own novel definition of the state as a monopoly of physical and symbolic violence following an autonomous state logic. In Chapter 5, his theory of the state is placed within his broader concept of field of power. In Chapter 6, we discuss Bourdieu's historical approach to state formation. Finally, in Chapter 7 we assess his theory of the state by examining its limitations and future empirical application.

---

[20] Steinmetz, George. *State/Culture: State formation after the Cultural Turn.* Cornell: Cornell University Press, 1999; Gorski, Philip. *The Disciplinary Revolution: Calvinism, Confessionalism and the Growth of State Power in in Early Modern Europe.* Chicago: University of Chicago Press, 2003.

CHAPTER 2

Bourdieu's Intellectual Biography

Abstract This chapter outlines Bourdieu's intellectual biography. It contends that his work can be understood in terms of a world-view. It then places his writings within the intellectual and political context within which they emerged. It argues that his work can be understood in terms of five major overlapping phases. Finally, it outlines and summarises his most important theoretical concepts, including habitus, field, capital, strategies and the economy of practices.

Keywords World-view · Habitus · Field · Capital · Practices · Symbolic power

Born 1st August 1930, in Lasseube, a small village in the South Western Pyrenees, the son of a peasant who subsequently became a postal worker, Bourdieu was raised in a Béarnese (a Gascon dialect) speaking home. After studying at the lycèe in Pau followed by the *Lycèe Louis-le-Grand* in Paris, he gained entrance to the prestigious *École Normale Supérieure,* where he studied an equally prestigious subject, philosophy. Following his *agrégation* in 1954, he began work teaching in a provincial lycèe in Moulin. In 1954, he started but later abandoned a thesis under the supervision of George Canguilhem on 'Temporal structures of affective life', before being reluctantly conscripted into the army in October 1955 and sent to Algeria during the Algerian War of Independence (1954–1962) at

© The Author(s) 2017
S. Loyal, *Bourdieu's Theory of the State,*
DOI 10.1057/978-1-137-58350-5_2

the age of 25. Posted in an air force unit of the military staff in the Chelif valley, he was later moved to the *Service de Documentation et d'Information* of the *Gouvernement* Général.[1]

After undertaking fieldwork and collecting information on the rural and urban context of Algerian life and society while travelling throughout the country, especially in Oran, Constantine, Mascara, Tlemcen as well as in the remote mountains of Kabylia, he eventually secured a position teaching sociology and philosophy at the University of Algiers in 1957. He returned to France in 1960 in order to work as an assistant to Raymond Aron at the Sorbonne. In 1961, he joined the faculty of letters in Lille as a lecturer in sociology, becoming director of a research group, the *Centre de sociologie européenne* (CSE). In 1964, he became *Directeur d'etudes as the École pratique des hautes études en sciences sociales* in Paris. In 1972, he published his groundbreaking work on kinship, ritual and social exchange based on his Algerian fieldwork, *Outline of a Theory of Practice.*[2] In 1975, he founded the journal *Actes de la recherche en sciences sociales* to promote the cause of a scientific sociology. In 1979, he published another major work which impacted heavily on the social sciences, *Distinction: A Social Critique of the Judgment of Taste.*[3] On the recommendation of Michel Foucault, he was appointed Professor of Sociology at the *Collège de France* in 1981. The 1980s also saw the publication of a number of other important works; the most relevant for the state include *Homo Academicus, Language and Symbolic Power* and *The State Nobility.*[4] He died on 23rd January 2002, from cancer.

---

[1] Yacine, Tassadit, 'Introduction' in Bourdieu, Pierre. *Algerian Sketches.* Edited by Yacine, Tassadit, Cambridge: Polity, 2013, p. 18.

[2] Bourdieu, Pierre. *Outline of a Theory of Practice.* 14th ed. Cambridge: Cambridge University Press, 1977.

[3] Bourdieu, Pierre. *Distinction: A Social Critique of the Judgment of Taste,* London: Routledge and Kegan Paul, 1984.

[4] Bourdieu, Pierre. *Language and Symbolic Power.* Cambridge: Polity, 1991; Bourdieu, Pierre. *Homo Academicus.* Cambridge: Polity Press, 1990; Bourdieu, Pierre. *The State Nobility: Elite Schools in the Field of Power.* Cambridge: Polity Press, 1998.

Sociology as a World-view

Drawing on the sociology of knowledge, it will be argued that Bourdieu's work can usefully be examined in terms of a 'world-view' expressing social, ethical and political interests which act as causal determinations affecting the content and coherence of his work. Such a theoretical manoeuvre permits us not only to understand some of the contradictions which occur within his copious writings but also to account for shifts in his sociological perspective and his attitude to a number of other theoretical approaches. In Bourdieu's case, his world-view is itself a dynamic one. His very early writings, especially some essays on Algeria, bear a strong imprint of Sartrean Marxism, though he was also heavily critical of that approach. Nevertheless, his world-view is that of a left republican/socialist.[5] Many of his analyses of Algeria, education and class express a critical engagement with the ideas and ideals of French republicanism and their instantiation, and deformation, in actual practice. In that regard, his political project bears striking parallels with the aloof form of scientifically and rationally grounded socialism of Durkheim, which had distinguished itself from Marxism by advocating a reformist and revisionist type of French republican-socialism led by Jaures. With Durkheim, Bourdieu shares an intellectual and evolutionary rather than revolutionary view of society,[6] the belief in a future socialist society based on the scientific and rational prognosis of its counterpart sociology, with its statistical and comparative findings, and that society required a powerful and active state albeit transformed from the current type.[7] There are many other parallels with

---

[5] Lane, Jeremy. *Bourdieu's Politics: Problems and Possibilities*. New York: Palgrave, 2006.

[6] As Lukes notes of Durkheim's politics: He had a 'faith neither in the activities of politicians in parliament nor in the possibilities of proletarian revolution; least of all did he believe in the internationalism of the working class' in Lukes, Steven. *Emile Durkheim: His Life and Work*. 2nd ed. United Kingdom: Penguin Books Australia, 1992, p. 322.

[7] As Clarke argues: 'After the Franco-Prussian war, the Third republic set itself the task of rebuilding France and it was on this basis that Durkheimian sociology with its promotion of a secular education had flourished. Durkheim's collectivistic, sociologistic, rationalistic, positivistic, and secular social philosophy centered on a secular state ensured that his thought became identified with the Republic as the embodiment of the collective conscience. Liberal republican intellectuals sought to

the work of Durkheim in addition to the Republican socialism, and an Enlightenment faith in the transformative potential of science and intellectuals. These include: the setting up of a journal to advance the cause of sociology *L'Anee Sociologique and Actes de la recherche en sciences sociales;* an emphasis on the social nature of classifications; foregrounding of education; that processes which in appearance stem from individual and psychological motives are actually the effect of social processes; that social transformations in society result from processes of social morphology – the structural relationships between individuals and an increase in dynamic density.[8]

By contrast, however, Bourdieu places considerably more weight than Durkheim on social class in his explanatory analysis and does not see the major malaise of modern societies deriving from anomie in the industrial and commercial sphere so that in this respect, his writings draw more heavily from a Marxist emphasis on class conflict. In this sense, Bourdieu's politics are perhaps closer to the younger generation of Durkheimians, including Mauss. Moreover, from the mid- to late 1980s in a context where neo-liberalism as a doctrine – entailing the entry of the market into unlimited social spheres, tropes of individual responsibility, the growing retrenchment of the social and protectionist state – becomes increasingly dominant in Western Europe and France in particular, Bourdieu's work becomes *explicitly* more political. Henceforth, Bourdieu becomes less concerned with providing an immanent and acerbic critique of French republicanism than in also defending its attributes of universalism and social equality in the face of this ideological onslaught.[9] But it is of

protect society as a whole by acting as a moral collective force aimed at transforming educational institutions into secular rationalist institutions to impose a morality on an anomic social order... The Durkheimian republicans found themselves positioned between a nationalistic Catholic and monarchist militarism seeking to overthrow the Republic on the one side, and a working-class increasingly taking on syndicalist forms seeking a transformation of the whole society on the other.' Clarke, Simon. *The Foundations of Structuralism: A Critique Levi-Strauss and the Structuralist Movement.* Sussex: Harvester, 1970, p. 11.

[8] See L. Wacquant 'Durkheim and Bourdieu: The Common Plinth and Its Cracks' in B. Fowler (ed.) *Reading Bourdieu in Society and Culture.* Oxford: Blackwell, 2000, pp. 105–120.

[9] For a discussion of Bourdieu's republican critique of culture see Yair, Gad. *The Last Musketeer of the French Revolution.* Plymouth: Lexington, 2009. For an

note that despite this overt shift from implicit interventions mediated through the scientific status of sociology to explicit forms of political engagement, all his work bears the mark of a political intervention of some sort.[10]

To speak of a world-view[11] is not to belittle or denigrate his work in a pejorative sense but to help us understand it and its underpinnings and implications more fully. Equally, it does not mean that his work should be flattened out on some political anvil. Bourdieu rightly argues that commentators that categorise his work in terms of one thinker – Marx, Weber or Durkheim – do so for polemical reasons.[12] It is more plausible to understand Bourdieu's sociological *oeuvre* by employing a framework he used in his study of Heidegger (1990). This saw Heidegger's work as the product of an overlap between two related semi-autonomous fields: the intellectual field and political field. This assessment, however, requires two connected qualifications. First, there is a sociological and epistemic reflexivity in Bourdieu's approach which, together with his fieldwork, provides the grounding for a social scientific analysis which is entirely missing from Heidegger's revolutionary conservatism. Consequently, Bourdieu's work rather falls within a third overlapping, semi-autonomous scientific field – which underpinned his idea of scholarship with commitment. Second, we need to understand the role that Bourdieu's personal and social trajectory played in shaping

overview of Bourdieu's political interventions see Poupeau, Franck and Thierry Discepolo. 'Scholarship with Commitment: On the Political Engagements of Pierre Bourdieu' in L. Wacquant (ed.) *Pierre Bourdieu and Democratic Politics: the Mystery of Ministry.* Cambridge: Polity, 2005, pp. 64–90; Bourdieu, Pierre. *Political Interventions: Social Science and Political Action.* Edited by Franck Poupeau and Thierry Discepolo. United Kingdom: Verso Books, 2008; and Lane, Jeremy *Bourdieu's Politics.*

[10] Poupeau, Franck and Thierry Discepolo. 'Scholarship with Commitment: On the Political Engagements of Pierre Bourdieu' in L. Wacquant (ed.) *Pierre Bourdieu and Democratic Politics: the Mystery of Ministry*, pp. 64–90; Bourdieu. *Political Interventions.*

[11] I take the concept from Mannheim.

[12] Bourdieu, Pierre. *In Other Words.* Cambridge: Polity, 1990, pp. 27–8.

his subsequent work while simultaneously avoiding what he calls the 'biographical illusion'.[13]

THE FRENCH INTELLECTUAL FIELD

As we shall see, Bourdieu's intellectual development draws heavily on the *sociological* work of Marx, Weber and Durkheim, using each to criticise and complement the insights of the other. But his overall theory is modified by the *anthropological* work of structuralism and based on the *philosophical* work of phenomenology, and later in the 1980s, the ordinary language philosophy of John Austin.

The post-war French intellectual field included within it both sociological and philosophical writers including the phenomenologists and existentialists, Husserl, Heiddegger, Merleau-Ponty and Sartre, as well structuralists, including Levi-Strauss, Dumezil, Braudel and Althusser, all of whom were to play an important role in shaping Bourdieu's work. His early education was as a philosopher and, as Decombes notes, the generation of philosophers in France between 1930 and 1960 were preoccupied by three dominant H's – Hegel, Husserl and Heidegger – while an older generation from the 1960s were more concerned with the three masters of suspicion – Marx, Nietzsche and Freud.[14] Hegel became especially prominent following Kojeve's anthropological reading of the master–slave dialectic in which the 'fight for recognition' becomes central for philosophy.[15] This struggle between humans for recognition where oppressors gain recognition by dominating and oppressing others, but ultimately in a contradictory and self-defeating way, played a major role in shaping Sartre's work as well as the writings of Fanon and Lacan. It also has an influence, albeit modified, on Bourdieu's philosophical anthropology.

Although Sartre was intellectually the dominant figure in French phenomenology, it is really Husserl, Heidegger and Merleau-Ponty who play

---

[13] Bourdieu, Pierre. *Sketch for a Self-Analysis.* Chicago, IL; London: University of Chicago Press, 2008.

[14] Descombes, Vincent. *Modern French Philosophy.* Cambridge: Cambridge University Press. 1981

[15] Kojève, Alexandre, *Introduction to the Reading of Hegel: Lectures on the 'Phenomenology of Spirit'.* Edited by Allan David Bloom. New York: Cornell University Press, 1980.

a more direct and significant role in the development of Bourdieu's thinking.[16] Husserl, who saw phenomenology as the descriptive, non-reductive science of what appears, especially through and in the subjective and inter-subjective medium of consciousness, attempted to provide a grounding for the conditions of possibility of objective knowledge, a philosophical account of conscious cognition which also discussed the environments, horizons or world (as the horizon of horizons) within which it functioned. Heidegger took phenomenology further by opening Husserl's phenomenological brackets and distinguishing between objects that were ready-at-hand (*Vorhanden*) to be used immediately in an unthinking way and those present-at-hand (*Zuhanden*) of a theorist or scientist looking at or observing something.[17] In Merleau-Ponty's work, a sharp distinction was made between the intentional or cognitive relation to objects, activity and space and a bodily 'motor' intentional understanding which contains a wholly divergent logical structure. Here, the body was not seen as an object in the world 'but as our means of communication with it, to the world not conceived as a collection of determinate objects, but as the horizon latent in all our experience and itself ever-present and anterior to every thought'.[18] The unreflexive bodily understanding of space and activity could be counterposed to reflexive, cognitive, intentional acts in terms of a spatiality of situation rather than position. Understanding was not through representations or articulations but contained in bodily memory, a pre-reflexive understanding, which was beyond an actor's consciousness and independent of his or her will.

Phenomenology, especially the Sartrean variety, was to be later challenged by structuralism, especially following the work of Levi-Strauss in the *Elementary Structures of Kinship* (1949) and *Tristes Tropiques* in 1955.[19] For Levi-Strauss, examining both kinship and myth, the way to move beyond positivism and humanism was by identifying an autonomous

[16] Bourdieu, *In Other Words*, p. 5.

[17] Heidegger, Martin. *Being and Time*. New York: Harper Row. 1962.

[18] Merleau-Ponty, Maurice. *The Phenomenology of Perception*. London: Routledge. 1962, p. 92.

[19] Levi-Strauss. 1949. *The Elementary Structures of Kinship*. Boston: Beacon Press, 1969; Levi-Strauss, Claude. 1955. *Tristes Tropiques*. London: Penguin, 2012.

order of reality, the symbolic order where cultural meanings inhere, and which exists prior to and independently both of the material world symbolised and the individuals who undertake the symbolisation. This objective meaning of the symbolic order existed in the unconsciousness, which mediates between people and the world and can be understood scientifically. Although structuralism and phenomenology are often regarded as dialectically opposed – structure against history, object against subject, unconscious versus conscious, determinacy versus free will, immanence to transcendence, philosophical versus anthropological – as schools they actually share a great deal in common. This is illustrated by the relatively seamless move of a number of thinkers from phenomenology and existentialism to structuralism such as Lacan, Foucault, Poulantzas[20] and Bourdieu.

Social and Political Context

Many of the arguments of the post-war French philosophers have to be situated in relation to the optimistic arguments of the Third Republic in which philosophy was seen as part of the mission of the state to foster Republican institutions.[21] Given restrictions of space, it is impossible to discuss these in any depth but only to point to some superficial markers. Post-war France under the watch of De Gaulle was characterised by a period of rapid economic boom following the introduction of high-technology modernisation but also effected by a number of crises entailing colonial wars in Indochina and Algeria, the latter stretching into the Fifth Republic. It was also a society characterised by enormous contradictions: on the one hand, immediately following the Second World War, a peasant class consisting of up to 45 % of the population; on the other, a country where cultural and literary production, and intellectual journals boomed, especially in the philosophical, literary and human sciences.[22] France's national ideological stance centred on equality and universalism, but it was a nation riven by class distinctions and rule over

---

[20] Clarke, *The Foundations of Structuralism*, p. 7.

[21] Ibid.

[22] Anderson, Perry. *The New Old World*. London: Verso, p. 140.

subjugated colonies. It was especially the latter, specifically the war in Algeria, as Le Sueur rightly points out, that shaped the work of a number of French intellectuals including Bourdieu.[23]

Although implicitly informed by his analysis of Algeria, it is in a later socio-political conjuncture that Bourdieu's work on the state emerges. His writings on the state began in the mid-1980s and as an attempt to reassert what he calls the 'left hand' of the state – the social aspects of the state tied to its universalism, public interests and the provision of welfare in the context of abruptly changing social conditions with the correlative increase in market liberalisation and rising neo-liberalism – an aspect of the 'right hand of the state'. Neo-liberalism, already a widespread and expanding global phenomenon by the 1980s, arguably took hold in France under Mitterrand's Socialist Presidency and its turn towards global financial markets from 1983 onwards.[24] It is in this sense that Bourdieu's writings on the state need to be read as much as a political intervention within the political field, as a theoretical intervention in the intellectual field.

Outlining Bourdieu's Work

Bourdieu's work, in the UK in particular, has been read as that of a *social* theorist who had also focused on reproduction of domination in education, culture, consumption and power. His association with social theory particularly was a result of an unhelpful preoccupation with conceptual discussions of the binaries of subjective and objective, agency and structure that characterised the increasingly specialised British sociological field during the 1980s and 1990s where *sociological* theory increasingly became an autonomous discipline labelled *social* theory. It is, however, more reasonable to see Bourdieu's sociology as always driven by specific empirical research questions, agendas and problems, albeit theoretically informed. It is in these empirical contexts of examining cultural dislocation, ritual practices, economic behaviours, education and schooling, art and literature that his concepts develop and evolve. And it is also as a result

---

[23] Le Sueur, James. *Uncivil War: Intellectuals and Identity Politics during the Decolonization of Algeria*, Philadelphia: University of Pennsylvania Press, 2001.

[24] Anderson, *Old New World*.

of being shaped by specific empirical contexts and redeployed in others that his concepts can sometimes appear contradictory.

Given his substantial output including almost 40 books and over 200 articles covering almost half a century, his *oeuvre* is not of one piece. It may be useful to draw attention to five major phases in his development to facilitate a heuristic and conceptual mapping of his work. These phases are not exclusive, but rather overlapping, reflecting a shift of emphasis in his work as he recursively elaborates on concepts that previously remained implicit, or draws and develops on others according to the empirical question at hand. They include: (1) An early phase on Algeria and the Béarn peasantry; (2) a second phase looking at education and class reproduction; (3) a third phase analysing practice and domination; (4) a fourth phase foregrounding symbolic power; (5) a final phase in which his work increasingly becomes an overt form of political intervention. Although divergent in a number of respects, all five phases focus on how actor's are perceived and perceive themselves, modes of domination, their dissimulation and reproduction within specific empirical domains.

Bourdieu's writing on the state are an extension and development of his broader sociological writings and his political world-view. It may therefore be useful to give a brief general outline of some of the key concepts informing his theory of practice, especially the concepts of habitus, field, capital, the economy of practices and epistemological reflexivity, within a review of the first four phases of his development.

1. Algeria and the Bearn Peasantry

Although not generally discussed[25] – partly because the concepts of habitus, field and capital remain absent – his writings on Algeria had a profound impact on his subsequent work.

---

[25] For exceptions see Lane, Jeremy. *Pierre Bourdieu*. London: Pluto, 2000; Calhoun, Craig. 'Pierre Bourdieu and Social Transformation.: Lessons from Algeria' *Development and Change*, 37(6). 2006, pp. 1404–1415; Goodman, Jane E. and Paul A. Silverstein (eds.) *Bourdieu in Algeria: Colonial Politics, Ethnographic Practices, Theoretical Developments*. Lincoln: University of Nebraska Press, 2009; Loyal, Steven. 'The French in Algeria, Algerians in France: Bourdieu, Colonialism and Migration' *The Sociological Review*, 57(3). 2009, pp. 406–427.

Bourdieu's decision to carry out systematic fieldwork into the harsh realities and brutal policy of 'pacification' and 'resettlement' by the colonial French authorities set him apart from other intellectuals writing on the war, both those who supported it and those opposed to it.[26] The charged situation of the war in which as many as 400,000 died[27] and as many as 2 million Algerians underwent some form of social upheaval precipitated his shift from philosophy to anthropology and sociology. Together with his work on the Béarn peasantry of his own childhood,[28] this intellectual transition provided the basis for the development of an epistemic reflexivity, allowing him to balance science and politics and to avoid the paradox in which 'good intentions so often make bad sociology'.[29] The emphasis on carrying out socio-political analysis but firmly anchored in a social scientific framework, in both a Weberian and Durkheimian sense, was to strongly mark his subsequent output. The work on Algeria which attempted to analyse how Algerian's fashioned by economic dispositions acquired in a pre-capitalist world attempted to adjust to a new colonially imposed world of capitalist dispositions, constituted a theoretical-cum political intervention in ongoing intellectual and policy debates extant at the time of the war, including those of Tillion, Sartre and Fanon. Moreover, right at the outset, his use of the sociological writings and ideas of Marx, Weber and Durkheim is evident though importantly, as we noted above, they are developed upon a prior philosophical understanding of the work of Husserl – on whose analysis of temporal structures he was writing his doctorate – and Merleau-Ponty's work on bodily perception.[30]

In his first book, *The Algerians* written in 1958, and reprinted and expanded in 1961 and 1962,[31] together with his work *Travail et travailleurs en Algérie* (Bourdieu et al. 1963), and *Le Déracinement* (1964) with Abdelmalek Sayad,[32] Bourdieu focuses primarily on revealing the universal

---

[26] Le Sueur. *Uncivil War.*

[27] Ibid., p. 1.

[28] Bourdieu, Pierre. 'Algerian Landing' *Ethnography*, 5(4). 2004, p. 438.

[29] Bourdieu, Pierre. *The Logic of Practice.* Cambridge: Polity Press, 1992, p. 5.

[30] See Bourdieu, *In Other Words*, pp. 6–7.

[31] Bourdieu, Pierre. *The Algerians.* Boston: Beacon Press. 1961.

[32] Pierre Bourdieu, Darbel, Alain, Rivet, Jean-Pierre, and Seibel, Claude. *Travail et Travailleurs en Algeria*, Paris and the Hague: Mouton, 1963; Bourdieu, Pierre

laws tied to acculuration, deculturation and cultural interpenetration – the spread of cultural values between the various groups as part of a 'kaleido-scopic mechanism'. Bourdieu notes how structural and cultural similarities lead groups to employ strategies aimed at constructing differences. What he would later refer to as 'group making'[33] involves agents actively pursuing a logic of distinction and differentiation. This pursuit of recognition and distinction constitutes a central dimension of his philosophical anthropology focusing upon recognition and misrecognition.[34] Expanding the discussion of cultural interpenetration and contagion by examining it in terms of a clash of civilisations between a traditional Algerian society 'that has always looked to the past for its ideal way of life'[35] and a dynamic forward-looking European civilisation, Bourdieu argued that the result was 'social, economic and psychological disaggregation'.[36] The enormous power difference between the two groups was to find expression through the rigid caste like relations between them. The extreme differences in power influenced the self-perception, or what he would later call the 'habitus', of all the actors concerned as dominated groups came to see themselves through the eyes of the dominant. Stereotypes of Algerians as uneducated and feckless, and of Europeans as holding positions of prestige and power, became generalised frameworks for interpreting one another's behaviour: 'the colonial system can function properly only if the dominated society is willing to assume the very negative nature or "essence" (the Arab cannot be educated, is impro-vident, etc.) that the dominating society holds up for it as its destiny'.[37] Bourdieu would later term such processes as 'symbolic violence'.

However, this process of self-identification and evaluation through the eyes of the more powerful was not a simple one-way process of domination but rather a complex and dialectical one, especially within the context of war. In a situation in which he attempts to understand the conditions of

and Abdelmalek Sayad. *La Deracinement: La crise de l'agriculture traditionanelle en Algeria*, Paris: Editions de Minuit, 1964.

[33] Bourdieu, Pierre. 'What Makes a Social Class? On the Theoretical and Practical Existence of Groups' *Berkeley Journal of Sociology*, 32, pp. 1–18.

[34] Bourdieu, Pierre. *Pascalian Meditations*. Cambridge: Polity Press, 2000.

[35] Bourdieu, *Algeria*, p. 94.

[36] Bourdieu, *Algerian Sketches*, p. 40.

[37] Bourdieu, *Algeria*, p. 134.

possibility of revolution, Bourdieu notes that discrimination, domination and widening inequality generated by colonial policy had led to a sense of resignation and fatalism amongst the Algerians, but it also resulted in resentment and revolt. Cultural interpenetration made social reflexivity possible: the arrival of a new European tradition allowed Algerians to evaluate and assess the value of their own traditions by way of contrast.

Studies on the Béarn Peasantry
Equally important to Bourdieu's intellectual development was research he carried out in his native Béarn on the fundamental changes affecting the peasantry during France's post-war boom, as seen through the prism of bachelorhood: 'bachelorhood is the privileged occasion to experience the wretchedness of the peasant condition'.[38] This research, first published in 1962, the same year as many of his articles on Algeria, also marked a further development in his intellectual framework and included the introduction of the concept of habitus, though used in a restricted sense. In parallel with Algeria, the focus was on the erosion of a rural way of life or ethos driven by capitalism and urbanism and the social, moral and psychological effects engendered by such a process. The central importance of land, its values centred on honour and authority relations were also discussed. Here, in Durkheimian terms, we see the disruption of a societal equilibrium as bachelorhood among the second eldest sons in the 'old society' shifts from being an exception, to becoming 'abnormal', and engendering *anomie* especially in large and poor families. Bourdieu again focuses on objective processes and how these are mediated, perceived and created through subjective understandings so that 'economic and social condition influences the vocation to marriage mainly through the mediation of the consciousness that men attain of that situation'.[39] Following Durkheim's analysis in *Suicide*, he also attempts to account for processes that are experienced and perceived as personal failings, as actually a consequence of broader social phenomena.

The Christmas ball held in a rural village – like French cultural imposition in Algeria – represents 'the scene of a real clash of civilizations'

---

[38] Bourdieu. *Algerian Sketches*, p. 93.
[39] Bourdieu, Pierre. *The Bachelors Ball: The Crisis of Peasant Society in Béarn.* United Kingdom: Polity Press, 2007.

through which 'the whole urban world, with its cultural models, its music, its dances, its techniques for the use of the body, bursts into peasant life'.[40] Specifically old style dances marked and bearing the peasant way of life in terms of their rhythms and names give way to urban dances from the towns. For Bourdieu, the body rather than consciousness becomes the locus of this shift, and it is this that bears the stamp of the old peasant way of life, rather than their temporal consciousness. As he notes, 'it is clear that the truly *empaysanit* ("empeasanted") peasant is not in his element at the ball'. Instead, like the uprooted peasantry of Algeria they experience 'the wretchedness of the peasant condition' in terms of an 'existence that has no present and no future'.[41] It is here that he first introduces the concept of *habitus* as 'a synthetic unity':

> Now, it is clear that the techniques of the body constitute systems, bound up with a whole cultural context.

This is not the place to analyse the motor habits characteristic of the Béarn peasant, the *habitus* that betrays the *paysanas*, the lumbering peasant. Spontaneous observation perfectly grasps the *hexis* that serves as a foundation for stereotypes. "Peasants in the old days", said an old villager, "always walked with their legs bowed, as if they had crooked knees, with their arms bent". To explain this attitude, he evoked the posture of a man wielding a scythe. However, the peasant is unable to meet the changing demands imposed on the body, by the Charleston or cha cha, for example, since bodily *habitus* is what is experienced as most "natural", that upon which conscious action has no grip'.[42] That is reshaping the techniques of the body or what he also terms, using the more traditional Aristotelian concept, 'hexis', is beyond their conscious control.

The work markedly bears the continuing imprint of Merleau-Ponty's phenomenology in focusing on both the actor's perception and self-perceptions but also on the role of the body. The bodily habitus becomes

---

[40] Ibid., p. 83.
[41] Ibid., p. 93.
[42] Ibid., p. 85.

so ingrained that the peasant becomes locked into it. To all intents and purposes habitus becomes fate.

2. Education and Social Reproduction

Bourdieu's work on schooling and education was to remain a consistent theme throughout his work featuring in numerous books including *Reproduction in Education and Society*, *Academic Discourse*, *Homo Academicus* and *The State Nobility*.[43] The central arguments concerning education and social reproduction are, however, most cogently and clearly expressed in his earliest work exploring these themes, *The Inheritors*, jointly written in 1964 with Jean-Claude Passeron whilst at the CES.[44] Composed at a time of rapid expansion in French higher education, the central concern of the book is the relation to culture of French university students and how this contributes to social inequality. Social classes, Bourdieu & Passeron note, are unequally represented in higher education where the children of workers make up only 6 % of the student population and where a senior executive's son is 80 times more likely to enter a university than a farm worker's son.[45] Not only are their hierarchies between universities, but there are also class differences within them. However, economic factors cannot solely account for such 'educational death rates'.[46] Rather cultural processes, which follow a similar logic to economic factors, are foremost. There is, according to Bourdieu, a strong elective affinity between the culture of school and higher education and the 'general culture' of the elite classes. Hence, educational culture is a class culture. Schools and universities presuppose previously gained

---

[43] Bourdieu, Pierre and Jean-Claude Passeron. *Reproduction in Education, Society and Culture*. 2nd ed. London: Sage, 1990; Bourdieu, Pierre, Jean Claude Passeron, Monique de Saint Martin, Richard Teese, Guy Vincent, and Christian Baudelot. *Academic Discourse: Linguistic Misunderstanding and Professorial Power*. Cambridge: Polity Press, 1996; Bourdieu, Pierre. *Homo Academicus*. *Cambridge: Polity. 1984*; Bourdieu, Pierre. *The State Nobility: Elite Schools in the Field of Power*. Cambridge: Polity Press, 1998.

[44] Bourdieu, Pierre and Jean-Claude Passeron. 1964. *The Inheritors: French Students and their Relation to Culture*. Chicago: University of Chicago Press, 1979.

[45] Ibid., pp. 1, 2.

[46] Ibid., p. 8.

cultural habits and social values themselves acquired through family background – the structure of language spoken, familiarity with culture in the
home, the theatre, galleries and concerts – extra-curricular culture which
together with educational certificates he will later term 'cultural capital'.
This capital is acquired by the dominant classes, and especially those
coming from Paris, largely implicitly through osmosis, rather than explicit
instruction. These 'socially conditioned predispositions' structure both
the students ease in assimilating school-transmitted culture and their
propensity to acquire it.[47] Through this affinity, the school and higher
education serve as social mechanisms of class reproduction while masking
that reproduction beneath the ideological veneer of individual talent or
giftedness.

This elective affinity between school and family culture also allows the
children of the middle classes to 'feel at home' in educational institutions
which is expressed in a confident self-belief in their giftedness and abilities
and manifest in the diversity and breadth of subjects they study and
cultural interests they adopt as well as their manner of elegance and
assuredness. Their family background has provided them not only with
'habits, skills and attitudes, which serve them directly in scholastic tasks
but also knowledge and know-how, tastes and "good-taste" whose scholastic profitability is no less certain for being direct'.[48] By contrast, those
students from the working class and lower middle class, who do not share
the same cultural past, feel out of place. Lacking the 'cultural hereditary' of
the elite, the latter's cultural habits and past serve as a handicap expressed
in terms of early ill-informed decisions and forced choices. The school
remains their only means for acquiring culture – which, using a term from
the early book on Algeria, is for them a form of distinctive acculturation.[49]

The differential objective opportunities for access result in different
subjective expectations of entering into higher education as something
'impossible' for the lower classes, 'possible' for the middle, and a 'natural'
future for the highest social classes, which in turn structure the jobs they
eventually take up. That is, all classes adjust their behaviour and subjective
expectations according to their objective chances.

---

[47] Ibid., p. 13.
[48] Ibid., p. 17.
[49] Ibid., p. 19.

As was the case in his earlier writings, broad social processes, and their effects, are perceived by those who experience them in terms of personal failings. Bourdieu also repeats his claims from earlier studies that the self-perception of the dominated is structured according to the values and word-view of the dominant social groups, and secondly that those from the lower classes participate in their own domination, fostering the reproduction of social inequality. Issues of culture, temporality, categorisation and self-perception, objective processes and subjective expectations, social processes interpreted through an individual lens, again all play key roles in this analysis. But in addition, Bourdieu also talks of how those who enter into the student system enter into a 'game with rules' almost akin to a Wittgensteinian language game embedded in a form of life.[50] The game analogy forms a central theme in his subsequent thinking.

3. Ritual and Social Practice

It was on the basis of this early fieldwork that Bourdieu developed his subsequent theoretical and empirical work on education, his studies of the Kabylia and social practice in *Outline of Theory of Practice* and the *Logic of Practice*[51] and his analysis of class and consumption in *Distinction*[52] as well as developing his key concepts of capital, strategies, reflexivity, recognition, field, and the economy of practices. The rationale underpinning these concepts is to overcome a number of oppositions that Bourdieu identifies as having plagued the social sciences, principally between subjectivism – how the constructed social world appears to individuals as in phenomenology – and objectivism – how the objective structures of the social world over and beyond individuals' perceptions structure and determine their actions as in structuralism. The concept of 'habitus' – a term with long intellectual pedigree going back to Aristotle, the scholastics, but also used in the work of Durkheim, Mauss, Husserl and Elias – is introduced in order to 'get out from under the philosophy of consciousness without doing away with the agent'.[53] Occupying a

---

[50] Wittgenstein, Ludwig. *Philosophical Investigations*. Oxford: Blackwell, 1957.

[51] Bourdieu, *Outline of a Theory of Practice*; Bourdieu, *The Logic of Practice*.

[52] Bourdieu. *Distinction*.

[53] Ibid., p. 14.

space between historical determinism and contingent future action, he defines habitus as 'durable, transposable *dispositions,* structured structures predisposed to function as structuring structures, that is, as principles which generate and organize practices'.[54] Habitus refers to dispositions which incline social agents to acts in determinate ways, without fully determining them. It can be usefully contrasted with Parsons's theory of socialisation. Rather than referring to explicitly taught values or rules that are consciously acquired or implanted in people's heads, these dispositions are unconscious or, at least, semi-conscious, they produce a social order without consciously following rules and they refer not to the mind but to the whole body. However, like processes of socialisation, these structured dispositions are acquired primarily in early childhood and form the sedimented basis upon which future experience and practices are shaped. Importantly, such dispositions reflect the social conditions of existence in which they have been acquired, becoming internalised through the body primarily through 'osmosis' within an environment. Hence, individuals from similar social or class conditions will share similar dispositions; they will tend to think, act and judge the social world in similar ways, as well as acquiring a similar practical sense of social situations, or a homogeneous 'feel for the game'. This includes semi-consciously calculating chances of success or failure terms of future actions, *anticipations,* gained through past experience, which are internalised and transformed into individual aspirations and expectations. Such dispositions are also durable and transposable in the sense they can be employed and adjusted to new and different situations and circumstances as they arise, thereby generating new actions and novel practices. Some critics have wrongly argued that Bourdieu's schema is deterministic.[55] His indebtedness to phenomenology proves this false. Bodily subjectivity and motor skills, as Merleau-Ponty argues, have the 'power to reckon with the possible';[56] for Bourdieu, they allow us to

---

[54] Bourdieu, *The Logic of Practice,* p. 50.

[55] Alexander, Jeffrey. 'The Reality of Reduction: The Failed Synthesis of Pirre Bourdieu' in Jeffrey Alexander. *Fin de Siecle Social Theory: Relativism, Reduction and the Problem of Reason.* London: Verso Books, 1995, pp. 128–217; Jenkins, Richard. *Pierre Bourdieu.* New York: Routledge, 1992.

[56] Merleau-Ponty, Maurice. *The Phenomenology of Perception,* Londson: Routledge. 2012. p. 112.

move beyond actual situations into future situations. Individuals are creative improvisers to the extent that they apply their acquired habitus, as embodied representations and practices, in new contexts and situations within determinate and shifting social contexts.

However, there is a sense in which his work does detract from the fully self-aware and conscious agent of, for example, Husserlian phenomenology and ethnomethodology. For Bourdieu, these imprints on the body remind us that we need to treat the body and the principles and cosmology it embodies, as beyond conscious manipulation.

The similar conditions of existence of a group or social class, especially in terms of their early upbringing, produce a homogenous group whose practices are harmonised without any conscious intention, or reference to a norm or explicit co-ordination. Despite the ability to adjust and improvise in situations, the habitus is a product of objective conditions and likely to undergo a *hysteresis effect* when it finds itself in an environment radically different from which it emerged. This can lead to dislocation but also to social conflict, as between different generations raised in different objective conditions, who possess different definitions of what is possible, impossible or probable.

According to Bourdieu, the concept of habitus can only be understood *relationally* in terms of what he calls social *fields*, the various social spheres and contexts within which agents act. The term 'field', which is only briefly discussed in *Outline* but more extensively in *The Logic of Practice* and through its empirical application elsewhere,[57] allows Bourdieu to move beyond visible interactions of symbolic interactionism to the concealed objective social positions that these agents occupy in the social world, or in his terminology, 'social space'. Fields refer essentially to the structure and patterning of social relationships:

> In analytic terms, a field may be defined as a network, or a configuration, of objective relations between positions. These positions are objectively

[57] Bourdieu, Pierre. 'The Force of Law: Toward a Sociology of the Juridical Field' *Hastings Journal of Law*, 38. 1987, pp. 814–853; Bourdieu, Pierre. 'Genesis and Structure of the Religious Field' *Comparative Social Research*, 13. 1991, pp. 1–44. Bourdieu, Pierre. *The Field of Cultural Production: Essays on Art and Literature.* Cambridge: Polity Press, 1993; Bourdieu, Pierre. *The Rules of Art: Genesis and Structure of the Literary Field.* Cambridge: Polity Press, 1996; Bourdieu, Pierre. *The State Nobility: Elite Schools in the Field of Power.* Cambridge: Polity Press, 1998.

defined, in their existence and in the determinations they have upon their occupants, agents or institutions, by their present or potential situation (*situs*) in the structure of the distribution of species of power (capital) whose possession demands access to the specific profits that are at stake in the field, as well as by their objective relation to other positions (domination, subordination, homology, etc.[58]

Fields develop historically and as societies diversify so more fields arise: 'the historic process is one of differentiation of the world into spheres'.[59] Such a view follows readily from Durkheim's social morphology, which points to increasing social differentiation, and dynamic density, as populations increase and societies develop. Fields take a variety of forms such as the educational field, economic field, the cultural field, the political field, the scientific field, the religious field etc. and can be further divided into sub-fields, the field of higher education for example. These fields shape and structure the actions of agents who enter into them, eliciting and triggering specific responses from agents with a particular habitus. Strictly speaking, economic and cultural power lie not in wealth or in educational titles but, in the relations between these forms and their associated fields of economic and educational relations.

Although each field has distinctive characteristics and unique logic or procedural rules, all fields contain or express certain universal properties. Firstly, they are semi-autonomous from each other, and thereby *relatively* impervious to the external influences and determinations of other fields – art is followed for art's sake, politics for power, action on the stock market for wealth, etc. Second, fields are 'fields of force', like magnetic fields, which attract and repel, they are characterised by tension and struggle, in which agents compete with one another to preserve or alter the constellation of positions that exists within the field. Consequently, fields can change and develop within the context of historical struggles. Fields – conceived as social fields of forces – solicit, instill and reproduce internal organizational criteria. Moreover, it is only in modern formations that autonomous fields have developed, become institutionalised and self-reproducing. According

---

[58] Bourdieu, Pierre and Loic Wacquant. *An Invitation to Reflexive Sociology.* Cambridge: Polity Press, 1992, p. 97.
[59] *On the State*, p. 75.

to Bourdieu, along with habitus, the concept of field enables him to transcend the dichotomy between reproduction and transformation, statics and dynamics, and structure and history.

Bourdieu's third key and inter-related concept is capital. This refers to any resource that enables people to appropriate profits from participating within specific fields. Bourdieu talks about a variety of forms of capital though he tends to focus on four main types: economic capital referring to money (including very high salaries), material and financial assets and private property; cultural capital refers to scarce symbolic goods, educational credentials and titles; social capital refers to social connections and profits accruing from group membership; and symbolic capital refers to recognition and prestige or the effects of any form of capital when they are not perceived for what they are, but are instead misrecognised. These capitals can also appear in various manifestations. Economic capital is generally *objectified* in goods or things, whereas cultural capital can be objectified in books, but can also take on an *embodied* state as dispositions of the mind/body, and an *institutional* state as rare educational qualifications.

For Bourdieu, a person's position in social space is determined by both the amount of capital they possess – the overall *volume,* and the type of capital they possess, the *composition* of their capital: 'The structure of the distribution of the different types and sub-types of capital at a given moment in time represents the immanent structure of the social world, that is, the set of constraints, inscribed in the very reality of the world, which govern its functioning in a durable way, determining the chances of success for practices'.[60] This distribution determines the agents' power and how they act within fields or different markets, or 'play' within various games:

> We can picture each player as having in front of her a pile of tokens of different colours, each corresponding to a given species of capital she holds, so that her relative force in the game . . . depend both on the total number of tokens and of the composition of the piles of tokens she retains, that is on the volume and structure of her capital.[61]

[60] Ibid., p. 242.

[61] Bourdieu and Wacquant, *Invitation*, p. 99.

People who play or participate in games within fields do so because they agree to do so, because they believe they have stakes or vested interests in the game, that is in terms of an *illusio*, that the game is worth playing.

Modifying Durkheim and Mauss's discussion of the social nature of the categories,[62] Bourdieu argues that the forms of categories and classifications are not only social, but also, embody power relations. Moreover, because of the direct and spontaneous correlation between social categories and social structures, they have the political effect of naturalising the social world.

This confusion of what is in fact a social and arbitrary order but which is perceived and understood as a natural and inevitable order entails *doxa*, which can be distinguished from orthodox or heterodox beliefs to the extent that the latter imply an awareness and recognition that different or contrary beliefs could exist.

Bourdieu develops his arguments concerning habitus, field and capital both in determinate empirical contexts, especially in analysing the logic of a gift and honour economy in Algeria, and in terms of a general science of the 'economy of practices'. In terms of the former and restating the importance of temporality, Bourdieu argues the structuralist approach, which sees gift exchange solely in terms of mechanical necessity, ignores the temporal structure of gift exchange which in fact 'defines the full truth of the gift'.[63] Gifts may not be returned either because of ingratitude or as an insult. 'In every society it may be observed that, if it is not to constitute an insult the counter-gift must be deferred and different, because the immediate return of an exactly identical object clearly amounts to a refusal'.[64] It is the lapse of time interposed between receiving and giving a gift that 'enables the gift or counter-gift to be seen and experienced as an inaugural act of generosity, without any past or future, i.e. without calculation'.[65] This time-lag, which consists of manipulating time or the tempo of action also allows us to introduce agents, their strategies and improvisation. An emphasis on practice, strategies, playing a game and the regulated

---

[62] Durkheim, Emile and Marcel Mauss. *Primitive Classification*. London: Cohen & West, 2009.

[63] *Outline*, p. 5.

[64] Ibid., p. 5.

[65] Ibid., p. 171.

improvisation of agents in place of reified, de-temporalised, abstract, static models based on 'mechanical laws' of the 'cycle of reciprocity' and pre-dictability means recognising that uncertainty is inherent in social life. Gift exchange is not a ritualised exchange but a confrontation of strategies.

In addition to his insightful discussion of temporality, Bourdieu in *Outline* also discusses what he calls an 'economy of practices'. Using the concept of economic in a wide sense, the framework implies that all practices – including economic, cultural, political, and scientific practices – aim at increasing or augmenting one's capital holding. That is, all practices are economic and cultural practices directed towards the maximising of material or *symbolic profits*, which follow an 'economic logic' in the broad sense of the term.

Within the contexts of fields and struggles, and according to their position in social space, actors employ 'strategies' to either maintain or improve their position. These strategies are not conscious strategies as in rational choice theory, but embodied strategies incorporated in the body as dispositions. The form the strategies take and the type of agent involved – individual, institutional or collective – is historically and socially deter-mined by the logic of the field. Human agents enter the field of struggle with historically given endowments, either in an *incorporated* state within the habitus as dispositions and competences, or in an *objectified* state as material goods. Two areas of especial importance for influencing a class habitus are family background in terms of father's occupation and family lifestyle, and the school in terms of qualifications as standardised markers of education since these provide sources of both economic and cultural capital. For Bourdieu, class is a central fact of modern societies. He also talks of 'strategies of reconversion' in which one form of capital may be converted for another. For example, economic capital may be used to fund private education to secure cultural capital. It is the mutual relation, correspondence or 'elective affinity' between habitus and field, mediated by capital, that generates social practice.

In *Outline of a Theory of Practice* and *The Logic of Practice*, Bourdieu discusses the different strategies and modes of domination that exist in pre-capitalist or traditional societies, and modern differentiated capi-talist societies, in a discussion that draws sparingly on Marx's *Grundrisse* (1973).[66] In traditional forms of society characterised by the absence of

[66] Marx, Karl. 1858. *Grundrisse: Foundations of the Critique of Political Economy.* London: Allen Lane, 1973.

a self-regulating market, a state, or an institutionalised education system, domination can only be maintained through strategies that need to be continually renewed in a personal and direct way through interactions. In addition, in pre-capitalist societies such as Kabylia, where overt brutal violence is collectively frowned upon, for example, between a master and his *khammes* (servants), such violence may lead the victim to flee or to initiate forms of counter-violence and effectively end the relationship of exploitation. Here, therefore, under the veil of enchanted relationships, symbolic violence predominates. This is 'the gentle, invisible form of violence, which is never recognized as such, and is not so much undergone as chosen, the violence of credit, confidence, obligation, personal loyalty, hospitality, gifts, gratitude, piety – in short, all the virtues honoured by the code of honour – cannot fail to be seen as the most economical mode of domination'.[67] As a hidden form of violence, symbolic violence involves gaining the 'consent' of the dominated to their own domination. Not only are the negative sanctions tied to overt violence and the censorship of direct personal interest stronger, but, economic capital is endlessly transformed into symbolic capital in order for the dominant to maintain their domination and to acquire the complicity of the dominated group. In such a context, domination must be euphemised and misrecognised by all concerned. An ethic of honour suits both the peasant–master as well as his khammes – through 'an honourable representation of his condition' in which the former treats the latter as an associate rather than servant.

By contrast, in modern capitalist differentiated societies where forms of capital have become accumulated, autonomous fields and social mechanisms institutionalised and objectified, power and domination are self-reproducing, masked and remain opaque. Symbolic violence is less dependent on being continually renewed through interpersonal relations but instead exists through institutional mechanisms such as education and philanthropy. Given the complexity and dissimulation entailed in such processes, the central role for sociology becomes to reveal the hidden mechanisms through which social domination reproduces itself.

Reflexivity

A further central feature of Bourdieu's sociological approach is its emphasis on epistemological reflexivity. The introduction of a systematic

---

[67] *Outline*, p. 192.

reflexivity constitutes a core factor in the foundation of any adequate social science. Rather than referring to a personal or narcissistic reflexivity, epistemological reflexivity enables sociologists to scientifically ground a sociological standpoint by scrutinizing what are taken as subjective and objective presuppositions in the social world. Stated briefly, for Bourdieu, it is not only the particular power relation between a Western anthropologist (Bourdieu) and the tribe or people he is studying (in this case the Kabylia) that needs to be acknowledged by the anthropologist, but *all* intellectual/academic forms of projection when studying human behaviour. Unreflexive intellectuals, writing from a standpoint characterised by *skole*, leisure or the 'scholastic point of view',[68] unvariably project their passive academic relation to the world onto their subjects and understand what for these subjects are practical practices, involving semi-conscious bodily activity, as a spectacle that needs to be decoded or interpreted, for example by recreating the meanings the actors employ in their activity.

In such a context the intellectual observer, given his or her subjective and objective relation to the world, is more concerned with the *opus operatum* of social actions than the *modus operandi*. A social scientific basis for the study of human behaviour crucially entails a break with 'scholastic reason' and involves a reflexive analysis of the social separation between the intellectual and his or her object of study. This reflexive moment must be included in all social analysis by subordinating 'all operations of scientific practice to a theory of practice and practical knowledge'.[69] It is only by instituting such a reflexive moment that one can bring to light the 'practical mode of knowledge in all practice'.

Although not discussed in great detail his theory of practice as elaborated in *Outline*, a central rationale underlying his whole approach is to establish sociology as an autonomous science as the ground upon which social criticism can unfold. In the *Craft of Sociology* written with Jean-Claude Chamboredon and Jean-Claude Passeron,[70] Bourdieu attempts to provide

---

[68] See Bourdieu, *Pascalian Meditations*.

[69] *Outline*, p. 4.

[70] Bourdieu, Pierre, Jean Claude Chamboredon, and Jean Claude Passeron. *The Craft of Sociology: Epistemological Preliminaries*. Germany: Walter de Gruyter & Co, 1991.

an epistemological grounding for the social sciences in general, and sociology in particular, which he develops in other work.[71] Drawing heavily on the historians of science Koyré, and Canguilhem, he argues that the philosophy of science generally overemphasises the importance of verification and validation at the expense of examining theory and hypotheses construction. Drawing on Bachelard he argues that the scientific act has to be won, constructed and confirmed. Epistemological facts contain a logical order initially entailing a break with ordinary concepts and phenomenal appearances, followed by the construction of hypotheses using a coherent theoretical model, and finally the testing of these hypotheses against this model. Such a process of winning, constructing and confirming facts takes place within the historical emergence of a semi-autonomous scientific field that is continually under threat from the external interests prevalent in other fields, including the economic field.[72]

4. Symbolic Power

An article on symbolic power, written in 1977, marks an important turning point and development in Bourdieu's work. In this condensed essay, he synthesises a number of heretofore divergent theoretical traditions and frameworks that deal with symbolism and language in an attempt to create a sociology of symbolic forms and power, entailing a conception in which power is less visible or misrecognised. Synthesising a neo-Kantian and idealist position that emphasises the productive activity of consciousness deriving from Cassirer, Sapir and Whorf, with the work of structuralists who emphasise the structured nature of language as a medium of communication, Bourdieu argues that symbolic power functions as a power of constructing social reality by establishing a *gnoseological* order (philosophical order of cognition), providing the immediate shared meaning individuals have of the social world. Here Durkheim's distinction between

---

[71] Bourdieu, Pierre. 'The Specificity of the Scientific Field of the Progress of Reason, *Social Science Information* 14(6). 1975, pp. 19–47; Bourdieu, Pierre. 'Animadversiones in Mertonem' in J. Clark, C. Modgil and S. Modgil (eds) *Robert K. Merton: Consensus and Controversy*, London: Falmer Press. 1990, pp. 297–301; Bourdieu, Pierre. *Science of Science and Reflexivity*. Cambridge: Polity, 2004.

[72] Bourdieu, *Science of Science*, p. xii.

logical and moral integration is of crucial importance. The former refers to the 'homogenous conception of time, space, number and cause, one which makes it possible for different intellects to reach agreement'. This in turn makes moral integration possible. Here there is a consensus on the meaning of the world 'which contributes fundamentally to the reproduction of the social order'.[73] Sense and consensus become tied. In a second synthesis, this is conjoined with Marxist and Weberian approaches that examine the political function of symbolic productions as instruments of domination and power, serving particular interests usually presented as universal interests. Henceforth, all relations of meaning and communication are seen inseparably as power relations that depend on the material or symbolic power that agents possess:

> It is as knowledge structured and structuring instruments of communication and knowledge that 'symbolic systems' fulfil their political function, as instruments which help to ensure that one class dominates another (symbolic violence) by bringing their own distinctive power to bear on the relations of power which underlie them and thus by contributing, in Weber's terms, to the 'domestication of the dominated'.[74]

The essay on symbolic power is Bourdieu's attempt to provide a less class reductionist account of ideological production without at the same time conferring the latter an absolute autonomy. Symbolic power is a power of making people see the social world in a specific way, of creating a vision of divisions that affirms or transforms the vision of the world that social agents possess, and therefore the social world itself. In his understanding of language, language, words, symbols are forms of action at a distance, 'an almost magical power which enables one to obtain the equivalent of what is obtained through force (whether physical or economic), by virtue of the specific effect of mobilization'.[75] For Bourdieu symbolic capital and power are a transformed or misrecognised form of other forms of power, that is, they depend upon the conversion of different types of capital-economic, cultural, political capital etc. into symbolic capital. Symbolic capital 'is any property (any form of capital

---

[73] Ibid., p. 166.

[74] Ibid., p.167.

[75] Ibid., p. 170.

whether physical, economic, cultural or social) when it is perceived by social agents endowed with categories of perception which cause them to know it and to recognize it, to give it value'.[76] Symbolic power and symbolic violence, by contrast, are exercised in an invisible way so that those beholden to them remain unaware of their very existence.[77] Symbolic violence and domination 'really begins when the misrecognition implied by recognition, leads those who are dominated to apply the dominant criteria of evaluation to their own practice'.[78]

The discussion of symbolic forms also point to the fundamental performative role played by language. The work of Austin on perfomatives and speech-acts,[79] or what Searle calls 'declaratives',[80] and on Anscombe's famous distinction between *cognitive states*, which describe the world and are derived from the facts of the world, and *conative states* which bring something about in the world, is central here.[81] Language and speech do not simply describe the social world but simultaneously constitute the very reality they describe.[82] Words, dictums and ritualised forms of expression

---

[76] *Rethinking the State*, p. 9.

[77] As a result, individuals: 'unwittingly contribute to wielding the symbolic violence that is wielded upon them, that is upon their unconscious, inasmuch as – and only inasmuch as – their mental structures are objectively in agreement with the social microcosm in which their specific interests are engendered and invested, in and by this very agreement' Bourdieu, Pierre. *In Other Words*, Cambridge: Polity, p. 12).

[78] Bourdieu Pierre and Boltanski, Luc. 'La Production de L'Ideologie Dominante' *Actes de la recherche en sciences social* Juin 3(3).1976, p8.

[79] Austin, John. *How to Do Things with Words*. Oxford: Oxford University Press, 1976.

[80] Searle, John. *The Construction of Social Reality*. London: Penguin. 1979.

[81] Anscombe, Elizabeth. *Intention*. Harvard: Harvard University Press. 2000; The work of Wittgenstein and Nelson Goodman is also directly of relevance. The latter discusses multiple worlds constructed differently according to the categories used by the observer. Goodman, Nelson. *Ways of Worldmaking*. Indianapolis: Hackett Publishing. 1978.

[82] It is important to note here, that unlike speech act theorists, language is not an autonomous realm of communication and meaning but integrally tied to power. As Wacquant notes, 'The efficacy of performative discourse is directly proportional to the authority of the agent who enunciates it and to its degree of congruence

are part of the symbolic struggles of everyday life, which imply claims to symbolic authority, which itself is a socially recognised power to impose a particular vision and division of the social world. For Bourdieu, the power of words is not to be located in the words themselves, but comes from 'outside' so to speak - from the institution that mandates and gives the individual the authority to speak. Social science is itself caught up in this struggle through the 'theory effect', 'which by helping to impose a more or less authorized way of seeing the social world, helps to construct the reality of that world'.[83] Language, theory, statements etc. operate, as Barry Barnes notes elsewhere, akin to a self-fulfilling prophecy.[84] Theories, descriptive and constative expressions and statements about a state of affairs are in fact performative discourses 'executing an action which attempt to bring about that very state of affairs or make individuals interpret and understand reality according to that discourse.'[85] Theory is thereby a programme of perception which contributes 'practically to the reality of what it announces by the fact of uttering it, of predicting it and making it predicted, of making it conceivable and above all credible and thus creating the collective representation and will which contribute to its production'. As a result 'one can modify social reality by modifying the agents' representation of it'.[86] Bourdieu argues that all science, even one that provides an 'objective measure of the degree of realism of the respec- tive positions' by 'describing the space in which these struggles take place and where what is at stake, among other things is the representation of the forces engaged in the struggle and their chances of success'[87] will also produce a theory effect. In this discussion Bourdieu vacillates rather problematically between a constructivism based on representation and constructing social reality and a realism based on a pre-given reality. Hence, for example, he argues that the theory effect is more powerful

with the objective partitions of society' Wacquant, *Pierre Bourdieu and Democratic Politics*, p. 15.

[83] Bourdieu, *Language*, p. 106.

[84] Barnes, Barry. 'Social Life as Bootstrapped Indiction' *Sociology* 17. 1983, pp. 524–545; Barnes, Barry. *The Nature of Power*. Cambridge: Polity. 1988.

[85] Bourdieu, *Language*, p. 128.

[86] Ibid.

[87] Ibid., p. 135.

'when the processes of objectification and of rendering things explicit are rooted in reality, and hence the divisions in thought correspond more precisely to real divisions'.[88]

He further argues that the social sciences must take the acts of naming and the rites of institution through which they are accomplished as an object of study. This involves examining the role of words in constructing social reality – as acts of constitution, and the struggle over social classifications in constructing classes of individuals based on age, sex, social position, but also social groups including clans, tribes, ethnic groups, and nations. These acts of naming are important as modes of 'group-making'.

Recognition and Misrecognition

Rather than his concept of cultural capital, for which he has become justly renowned, it is the concepts of symbolic power and symbolic capital – which became increasingly foregrounded in his work as it developed and where the concepts of recognition and misrecognition are to be found-that constitutes the core of his approach. The latter concepts underpin his entire *oeuvre*. They are constructed as part of his philosophical anthropology in which humans require recognition from others in order to justify their otherwise meaningless, contingent and finite existence. This existentialist vision of humans, and their desire to emerge from their absurd, indifferent existence and give meaning to life and death by participating in society, is discussed in one of his last major works, *Pascalian Meditations*.[89] But the theme of recognition and misrecognition, of how groups are seen and thereby see themselves, is also present at the outset, in his work on Algeria. As we noted earlier, the concepts of recognition and misrecognition were common currency in France in the 1950s and 1960s, drawn

---

[88] Ibid. Here if he argues that beliefs constitute the social world viz-a-viz performativity of language then how can they be measured according to an objective reality independent of it? It is impossible to collectively define beliefs as true or false (or real and unreal) objective or not, when these beliefs do not exist independently of what they are referring but are instead partially constitutive of that very objective reality. There is no criterion by which to judge them – that is, as Wittgenstein remarks elsewhere, 'there is no standard of correctness' Wittgenstein, *Philosophical Investigations* para 130.

[89] Bourdieu, *Pascalian Meditations*, pp. 237–245.

from the work of Hegel via Alexandre Kojève, and deployed in the work of a number of thinkers including Sartre, Fanon, Lacan and Althusser. They are also clearly evident in *Distinction* where individuals aim to differentiate themselves through distinction and pretension strategies through consumption. Similarly, in his writings on the state, where symbolic processes take centre stage, individuals strive to become consecrated and acquire identities through state nomination, categorisation and titles. That is they aim to become recognised and validated by the supreme social entity, a collectively alienated objectification that is akin to a god, the state. In the context of discussing Kafka's trial, he notes the importance of esteem and honour from other social actors:

> As in *The Trial*, where the slander is present from the first phase, the most categorical categoremes are there, from the beginning, from entry into life, which – and Kafka, a Jew in Prague, knew this well – starts with an assignment of identity designating a category, a class, an ethnic group, a sex or, for racist eyes 'a race'. The social world is essentialist, and one has that much less chance of escaping the manipulation of aspirations and subjective expectations when one is symbolically more deprived, less consecrated or more stigmatized, and therefore less well placed in the competition for the 'esteem of men', as Pascal puts it, and condemned to uncertainty as to one's present and future social being, which vary with one's power or impotence. With investment in a game and the recognition that can come from cooperative competition with others, the social world offers human beings that which they most totally lack: a justification for existing.[90]

[90] Bourdieu, *Pascalian*, pp. 238–239. He adds: 'So without indulging in the existential exhaltation of '*sein-zum-Tode*', one can establish a necessary link between three indisputable and inseparable anthropological facts: man is and knows he is mortal, the thought he is going to die is unbearable or impossible for him, and, condemned to death, an end (in the sense of *termination*) which cannot be taken as an end (in the sense of a *goal*), since it represents as Heidegger put it, 'the possibility of impossibility', he is a being without reason for being, haunted by the need for justification, legitimation, recognition. And as Pascal suggest, in this quest for justifications for existing, what he calls 'the world' or 'society' is the only recourse other than God. Ibid., p. 240.

As we shall see, it is the state which is the central bank for symbolic capital and therefore the site *par excellence* of social struggle. Having examined some of Bourdieu's key concepts, we can now turn to examine some of theories of the state that he selectively engages with.

CHAPTER 3

Classical and Modern Theories of the State

Abstract This chapter argues that in order to understand Bourdieu's theory of the state, we need to place it in the context of earlier classical and modern theories of the state. To that end, the classical theories of Marx, Weber and Durkheim are outlined in addition to modern theories that Bourdieu draws upon and refutes including Elias, Tilly and Corrigan and Sayer.

Keywords Marx · Weber · Durkheim · Elias · Tilly · Theories of state-formation

In order to understand Bourdieu's theory of the state, it needs to be situated in relation to both the classical theories – Marx, Weber and Durkheim and some modern theories of the state including that of Elias, Tilly and Corrigan and Sayer.[1]

In *On the State*, Bourdieu reviews, appraises and criticises all these theories with the exception of Durkheim, which is surprising, given that it is Durkheim's theory of the state that his own theory has the strongest affinities with. There are also strong parallels with Foucault's later work on

[1] Bourdieu also reviews the work of Eisenstadt, Anderson, and Barrington-Moore, and draws on the work Marc Bloch, Karl Polanyi, Wittfogel, Coulborn though fails to review Durkheim and Foucault whose theories share family resemblances with his own.

© The Author(s) 2017
S. Loyal, *Bourdieu's Theory of the State*,
DOI 10.1057/978-1-137-58350-5_3

the state. However, it should be noted that his selective use of secondary authors underlines the fact that Bourdieu's main intention is not to supply an extensive or detailed overview of extant theories. Rather, he is engaged in the more parsimonious project of detailing the emergence of an autonomous and powerful state logic and its impact on other aspects of the social world.

MARX

A coherent and systematic theory of the state remains elusive in Marx's writings. Instead, one finds different emphases and discussions pitched at different levels of abstraction – sometimes contradictory and discontinuous – about the nature of the state, scattered throughout his *oeuvre*. These, *inter alia*, see the state variously as acting as an instrument of bourgeois rule, distinguishing its ideological appearance as serving the general interests of society as a whole from its particular interest in serving capital, as constituting a relation of production, acting as a guarantor of capital accumulation, expressing the space within which class struggles unfold, and maintaining the social order and protecting private property.

In his early *A Critique of Hegel's theory of Right* (1843), which takes the Prussian state as background, Marx draws heavily on philosophical language of Feuerbach to argue that Hegel inverts the relationship between subjects and predicates, making the state a hypostatised abstraction. Hegel's separation of the state as the sphere of general, public and universal interest and civil society as the arena of private, self and egotistical interest does not reflect an inevitable process but expresses a definite historical period of commerce, and class formation. In this sense, the modern state as a separate, estranged entity outside of a civil society is a thoroughly unique institution wherein formal rule differs from the personal rule characteristic of Medieval society:

> The political constitution as such is brought into being only where the private spheres have won an independent existence. Where trade and landed property are not free and have not yet become independent, the political constitution too does not yet exist. The Middle Ages were the democracy of unfreedom. The abstraction of the state as such belongs only to modern times, because the abstraction of private life belongs only to modern times. The abstraction of the *political state* is a modern product.[2]

---

[2] Marx, *Critique of Hegel's Philosophy of Law*, pp. 31–32.

The abstraction of the state presupposes the abstraction of the individual, of formally equal individuals shorn of all determinations including their concrete economic inequalities.[3] By arguing on the basis that the state pursues the general interest transcending the particular private interests of civil society, Hegel is in fact sanctioning its role in supporting economic inequality.

For Marx, the fundamental role of the state is to defend property, especially inherited land rationalised through primogeniture. The notion of a bureaucracy serving the universal and general interest remains an ideal abstraction in contrast to material concrete personal interests of civil society. The modern state not only presupposes a division between the abstract private individual and the public citizen but, also, as Sayer rightly notes, the separation of the 'institutions of ruling from the person of rulers'.[4] In contrast to feudalism, the bourgeoisie as the dominant class do not wield state power directly but do so through the mediation of a state bureaucracy. Rather than transcending the egoistic private interests inherent in civil society, for Marx, the bureaucracy, as the formalism of the state, actually expresses them. It develops its own corporate interests, and itself becomes the ultimate purpose of the state by operating in a dialectical relationship with the individual interests pervading civil society. Here the 'aims of the state are transformed into aims of bureaus, or the aims of bureaus into the aims of the state'. As part of a rigid bureaucratic machine, in which bureaucrats passively obey orders, the state pays their salaries, which makes them pursue their own interests including promotion: 'The bureaucracy has the being of the state, the spiritual being of society, in its possession; it is its private property. The general spirit of the bureaucracy is the secret, the mystery, preserved inwardly by means of the hierarchy and externally as a closed corporation ... As far as the individual bureaucrat is concerned, the end of the state becomes his private end: a pursuit of higher posts, the building of a career'.[5]

---

[3] 'In order to attain universal equality of a "common interest", society is compelled to abstract from its real divisions and deny them value and significance ... One obtains the *citizen* only by abstracting from the bourgeois'. Ibid., p. 35.

[4] Sayer, Derek. *Capitalism and Modernity: An Excursus on Marx and Weber*. New York: Taylor & Francis, 1990, p. 77.

[5] Marx, *Critique*, p. vii.

Marx continues many of these discussions, concerning the separation of state and civil society in the *German Ideology* where the state constitutes a form in which ruling interests are asserted as universal interests.[6] He also brings in a broader discussion of division of labour and private property and sees them as playing a fundamental role in the emergence of the state and as representing two sides of the same coin. In more empirical and less philosophical works such as *The Eighteenth Brumaire* and the *Civil War in France* (1852), discussions concerning the state are more firmly rooted within a class and historical materialist analysis. *The Eighteenth Brumaire of Louis Bonaparte* sees the state as having acquired a level of autonomy within the context of a temporary equilibrium in class struggles, emphasising the importance of the state's role in maintaining social order in facilitating bourgeois domination.[7] In *the Civil War in France* (1871), he defines the state as a centralised 'power, with its ubiquitous organs of standing army, policing, bureaucracy, clergy and judicature'.[8] Both works emphasise the degree of autonomy that the state has acquired in France under the dictatorial Bonapartist regime following Louis-Napoleon Bonaparte's coup d'Etat in 1851.

These increasingly nuanced discussions of class can be contrasted with more simplistic comments and aphorisms in the *Communist Manifesto* (1848), where the state in shorthand is 'a committee for managing the affairs of the bourgeoisie'.[9] And in Marx's famous 1859 *Preface to a Contribution to the Critique of Political Economy*, it is reduced to a superstructure, built upon the 'real foundation' of the economic structure of society.[10] Such an interpretation merged with Engels discussion of the state in the *Origins of Private Property and the State (1884)*,[11] which in turn had a strong impact on

---

[6] Marx, Karl and Frederick Engels. 1846. *The German Ideology*. New York: Prometheus Books, 1998.

[7] Marx, Karl. 1852. The Eighteeneth Brumaire of Louis Bonaparte in Karl Marx *Collected Works*, 11.

[8] Marx, Karl. 1871. 'The Civil War in France' in D. Fernbach (ed.) *Karl Marx the First International and After*, Harmonsworth: Penguin, 1973, p. 217.

[9] Marx, Karl and Engels, Frederick. 1848. *Manifesto of the Communist Party*, in *MECW 6*, p. 486.

[10] Marx, Karl. 1859. *Preface to a Contribution to a Critique of Political Economy*. London: Lawrence and Wishart, 1971.

[11] Engels, Frederick. 1884. *The Origin of the Family, Private Property and the State*. London: Penguin, 2010.

the writings of Lenin – who viewed the state as 'special bodies of armed men, prisons etc'.[12] – and the Second International, where the state is depicted not as an independent entity but merely as an instrument of class rule, an administrative force of coercion facilitating the exploitation of wage-labour or expressing the domination of the bourgeoisie in the political sphere.

More recently, during the 1970s, disputes concerning the nature of the state led to a rather fruitless debate between Ralph Miliband and Nicos Poulantzas[13] centring on the question of state autonomy. That is, the focused on whether the state was an instrument of class rule or whether it possessed a relative autonomy from political economy and class relations.

Given such a variety of interpretations of the state by Marx, it is probably more apposite to understand his different emphases and descriptions of the state within the context of his method of abstraction.[14] Here the state needs to be reconstituted in complex concrete analyses that examine its generic role both in maintaining the social order and cohesion and promoting capital accumulation.[15]

In a highly reductive, unsympathetic and circumscribed view of Marxism, Bourdieu argues, that Marx and Marxist interpretations of the role of the state are especially problematical. In addition to its economism, Marxism entails a 'pessimistic functionalism' as opposed to the 'optimistic functionalism' of structural-functionalist theories. Such functionalism, however, lacks a description of the mechanisms needed to fulfil the functions they posit: 'from Marx to Gramsci, to Althusser and beyond, it always insists on characterizing the state by what it does, and for the people for whom it does what it does, but without investigating the actual structure of the mechanisms deemed to produce its foundations . . . the question of the being and acting of this thing designated as

---

[12] Lenin, Vladimir. 1918. *The State and Revolution*. Chicago: Haymarket, 2014, p. 45.

[13] Miliband, Ralph. 'The Capitalist State – Reply to Nicos Poulanzas' *New Left Review*, 59, 1970; Miliband, Ralph. *The State in Capitalist Society: The Analysis of the Western System of Power*. London: Quartet Books, 1973; Miliband, Ralph. 'Poulantzas and the Capitalist State', *New Left Review*, 82. 1973; Poulantzas, Nicos. 'The Problem of the Capitalist State'. *New Left Review*, 58. 1969; Poulantzas, Nicos, 'The Capitalist State: A Reply to Miliband and Laclau' *New Left Review*, 95. 1976; Poulanzas, Nicos. *State, Power, Socialism*. London: New Left Books, 1978.

[14] Jessop, Bob. *The Capitalist State: Marxist Theories and Methods*. Oxford: Martin Robertson.1982; Sayer, Derek. *The Violence of Abstraction*. Oxford: Blackwell.

[15] Jessop, *The Capitalist State*, p. 24.

the state is sidestepped'.[16] Although he disagrees with this restricted form of functionalism, this does not mean Bourdieu eschews a view of the state as fulfilling some of the functions that Marxists ascribe to it, such as the production of consent. However, the question of whether the state has autonomy pursued by Miliband and Poulantzas, for example, is deemed a false one, this is rather an empirical question: 'instead of asking whether the state is dependent or independent, you examine the historical genesis of a policy, how this happened, how a regulation, decision or a measure was arrived at, etc. You then discover right away that the academic *Streit* [dispute] between dependence and independence has no meaning, that it is impossible to give a response that is valid for all circumstances'.[17] As we shall see, Bourdieu intends to by-pass this dilemma, as well as the Weberian view of the absolute autonomy of the state, with his view of the state as a bureaucratic field, which like all fields is semi-autonomous with its own specific logic, state capital and normative dimension.

In addition, although Marxists allocate a prominent role to ideology for maintaining the social order, and reproducing the *status quo*, this, for Bourdieu, either presupposes a Cartesian focus on individuals' and their consciousness[18] or depends on a base superstructure model where the ideological superstructure is determined by an economic base. Such a view needs to be rejected, or at least reversed so that the symbolic realm predominates.[19]

WEBER'S THEORY OF THE STATE

Weber's discussion of the state is in some ways more systematic and developed than Marx's, yet it nevertheless remains incomplete and inconsistent. Drawing heavily on the *Staatstheorie* of Jellinek, Treitschke, Gottle and

---

[16] Bourdieu, *On the State*, p. 5.

[17] Ibid., p. 112.

[18] Bourdieu, Pierre and Eagleton, Terry. 'Doxa and the Common Life (In Conversation Pierre Bourdieu and Terry Eagleton' *New Left Review*. 191. 1992, p. 113).

[19] Bourdieu writes: 'forms of domination, which a certain philosophical tradition calls symbolic, are so fundamental that I find myself wondering whether a social order could function, even in its economic foundations, without these forms of domination. In other words the old model of infrastructure and superstructure... must be rejected, or, if you insist on keeping it, must at least be turned upside down' Bourdieu, *On the State*, p. 161.

Rathenau, the state emphatically occupies a more central place in his thought than that of Marx. Yet, like Marx, in his early writings at least, the material backdrop is the Prussian state, though in this instance interpreted through Weber's distinctive liberal-nationalist worldview.

Rather than talking about the state *per se*, Weber discusses many different forms of state – a 'robber state', a 'welfare state', a 'constitutional state', a 'culture state' and even a 'patrimonial state'.[20] There are also subsequent changes of emphasis and criteria delimiting the state in his writings – from emphasising its monopoly of physical force, rulership and legitimacy, to the state as a machine following a process of occidental rationalisation, to the state as a producer of value ideas, a legal order or rational bureaucratic enterprise.[21] Weber therefore not only describes the state as a locus of physical force but also its political, institutional and organisational nature, encompassing legitimation, administrative staff and social order, in addition to seeing it as the 'most constitutive element in all cultural life'.[22] Given this plethora of functions and activities,[23] it is difficult for Weber to provide a clear-cut definition of the state, since there are few activities that the state has not been involved in. Nevertheless, what remains consistent in his discussions of the state is that it is primarily a relationship of force and rule of material and ideal interests.[24] Power *(Macht)* – the ability to impose one's will despite opposition from others and to use one's organisational might to control the action of others – and

---

[20] Weber, Max. *Economy and Society: An Outline of Interpretive Sociology.* 2nd ed. Edited by Guenther Roth. Berkeley, CA: University of California Press, 1978. Volume II, p. 902, 106.

[21] Anter, Andreas. *Max Weber's Theory of the State: Origins, Structure, Significance.* London: Palgrave, MacMillan, 2014.

[22] Weber, Max 'The objectivity of knowledge in social science and social policy' in Sam Whimster (ed.) *The Essential Weber.* London: Routledge, p. 371.

[23] M. Weber, *Economy and Society*, p. 54. In his lecture on 'Politics as a vocation' he adds: 'There is hardly a task which has not been undertaken by some political association at some time or other, but equally there is no task of which it could be said that it is always, far less *exclusively*, the preserve of those associations which are defined as political (in today's language: states) or which were the historical predecessors of the modern state'. Weber, Max. 1919 'Politics as a vocation' in *Max Weber: Political Writings.* Edited by Peter Lassman. Cambridge: Cambridge University Press, 1994, p. 310.

[24] Anter, *Max Weber's Theory of the State*, p. 46.

Herrschaft combine so that states are intrinsically connected with domination. For Weber, these historically shifting forms of domination tend to persist, structurally crystallising around the economic, cultural and political dimensions of the social world. Hierarchical forms of social stratification are expressed in the interdependent conflicts of class, status and party. The manner in which states have acquired obedience thereby constitutes a central concern in his writings.

The multiplicity and changing nature of the ends of the state implies that the state can only be defined as a concept in terms of its means, eschewing a systematic outline of its aims and ends other than those broadly political and cultural, and tied to the maintenance of social order. These means primarily entail violence employed within a territory:

> In the last analysis the modern state can only be defined sociologically in terms of a specific means (*Mittel*) which is peculiar to the state, as it is to all other political associations, namely physical violence (*Gewaltsamkeit*). "Every state is founded on force (*Gewalt*)", as Trotsky once said at Brest-Litovsk... we have to say that a state is that human community which (successfully) lays claim to the monopoly of legitimate physical violence within a certain territory.[25]

This is an *ideal type* definition that involves distilling what states share in common. Although violence and force is not the only means employed by the state, it is the means *specific* to the state and it alone possessed the *right* or claimed the *legitimacy* to use physical violence. As he notes in another definition given in *Economy and Society*: 'the claim of the modern state to monopolize the use of force is as essential to it as its character of compulsory jurisdiction and of continuous operation'.[26] Such a monopoly remained absent during the Middle Ages. Monopolisation of force entailed the development of sovereignty, as two sides of the same coin.[27] In parallel with the development of capitalist enterprise via the expropriation of independent producers, the modern state is 'set in motion

---

[25] Ibid., pp. 310–311.

[26] Weber, *Economy and Society*, p. 56.

[27] As Anter argues, Weber: 'interprets and assesses the emergence of the modern state as a process of centralization, monopolization and statalisation, of ordering functions that had hitherto been exercised by decentralized instances' Anter, *Weber's Theory of the State*, p. 16.

everywhere by a decision of the prince to dispossess the independent "private" bearers of administrative power who exist alongside him'.[28] It is by dispossessing those who formerly owned the means of administration and means for war – 'the estates' – that the modern state comes into existence: 'thus in today's "state" (and this is fundamental to the concept), the separation of the material means of administration from the administrative staff, the officials and the employees of the administration, has been rigorously enforced'.[29] Later, the prince is replaced by party leaders so that there occurs an expropriation of the political expropriator in which party leaders, through usurpation or election, gain command of the political administration and derive their legitimacy 'from the will of the ruled'.

In order to carry out organised rule, the state requires an administrative apparatus and administrative staff, and the material means of administration. Hence, in addition to force and rule, the modern state is able to claim a monopoly of legitimate violence with the aid of a regularised administrative staff, as well as a paid army, over a delimited territorial area.

This allows Weber to give a compound definition of the state:

> the modern state is an institutional association of rule (*Herrschaftsverband*) which has successfully established the monopoly of physical violence as a means of rule within a territory, for which purpose it unites in the hands of its leaders the material means of operation, having expropriated all those functionaries of "estates" who previously had command over these things in their own right, and has put itself, in the person of its highest embodiment, in their place.[30]

Within a process of political expropriation led by monarchs, there emerged in the West, professional full-time functionaries who, as either prebendaries (bureaucrats provided a living) or salaried officials, singularly and exclusively served the prince within the context of their political struggles within dynastic political formations. This provided them both a material living, but more importantly, also gave them 'an ideal content for their

---

[28] Weber, *Politics as a vocation*, p. 315.

[29] Ibid.

[30] Ibid., p. 316.

own lives',[31] an inner meaning and purpose and devotion so that they lived not so much *from* politics but, *for* politics.

In a context where princes were first and foremost knights who fought rather than specialists in rule, and where the refinement of legal processes necessitated the work of trained lawyers, specialist functionaries became increasingly demanded. In these areas, specialised officialdom became the norm in the more advanced states in the West by the 16th century. The recruitment of professional officials by princes took place in a context of power struggles with estates in which the prince drew upon politically usable but unstable strata not belonging to the estates, including: a celibate literate clergy, who 'stood outside the machinations of normal political and economic interests';[32] men of letters with a humanist education; courtly nobility; and jurists with a university training. As Weber notes in relation to the latter: 'There is no clearer evidence of the powerful long-term effects of Roman law, as transformed by the late Roman bureaucratic state, than the fact that trained jurists were the main bearers everywhere of the revolutionary transformation of the conduct and the organization (*Betrieb*) of politics, in the sense of developing it in the direction of the rational state'.[33] The professions to which members of the French assembly belonged contained few bourgeois entrepreneurs or proletarians but masses of jurists. The modern state advocate and modern democracy therefore 'belong together'. In terms of their 'true calling', officials, unlike political leaders do not engage in politics or fight, but impartially administer. This process has led to the growth of a modern officialdom: a body of technically qualified, specialised, intellectual workers who had undergone long years of training and preparation for their role and who embodied a sense of honour prioritizing integrity.

States are for Weber, relationships of rule (*Herrschaft*) with one group of human beings ruling over another, dominant and dominated. For Weber, domination 'as the probability that certain specific commands (or all commands) will be obeyed by a given group of persons' also entails that 'every genuine form of domination implies a minimum of voluntary

---

[31] Ibid.
[32] Ibid., p. 327.
[33] Ibid., p. 328.

compliance, that is, an *interest* (based on ulterior motives or genuine acceptance) in obedience'.[34] In such a context: 'For the state to remain in existence, those who are ruled must *submit* to the authority claimed by whoever rules at any given time'.[35] Three grounds underpin this submission to authority through legitimation: 'traditional rule' exercised by the patriarch or prince of old, drawing on the authority of the past or of custom; 'charismatic rule' based on the 'the gift of grace', which refers to devotion, belief and trust in the exceptional leadership qualities and charisma of an individual – a prophet, a chosen war-lord or a great demagogue; and 'legal rule' through belief in the validity of statutes and juridical 'competence' deriving from rational rules. This is the rule exercised by the bureaucracy as the 'modern servant of the state'.[36] Individuals submit to the state not only because of fears of revenge from magical or real powers – but also of hopes – rewards in this life or the next, which dispose individuals to obey rulers.

Two additional features of Weber's theory of the state which are often overlooked need to be mentioned. First, Weber had defined the secular power of the state's monopoly of force in relation to the 'hierocratic' spiritual domination and monopoly of the church, 'which enforces its order through psychic coercion by distributing or denying religious benefits ("hierocratic coercion"). The monopolization of spiritual salvation and the role of religion are highly significant in terms of complementing the monopolization of physical force'.[37] Second, the three 'internal' forms of legitimacy and their corresponding organisational forms of domination are supplemented with a discussion of geopolitics, imperialism and nationalism. For Weber, a state's position of power prestige – based on nationalism and imperialism – in the geopolitical context is important for securing legitimacy within the state. As Collins notes: 'The legitimacy of state rulers and the state's tendency toward imperialist expansion are reciprocally related. A theory of imperialism is an integral part of a theory

---

[34] Weber, *Economy and Society*, p. 212.

[35] Ibid., p. 311.

[36] These constitute three ideal types of rule rarely found as pure forms in reality but, rather in their admixture.

[37] See Turner, Bryan. *Religion and Modern Society*. Cambridge: Cambridge University Press. 2011.

of domestic legitimacy and domestic political domination and vice versa'.[38] The groups who fight within the state for this power and legitimacy are differentiated according to class, status and party.

Many modern writers including Mann,[39] Poggi,[40] Skocpol[41] and Tilly[42] have drawn sparingly upon Weber's theory of the state as an organisational form. Here administrative, legal, extractive and coercive forms constitute core features of the state that operate in transnational contexts. Skocpol defines the state as 'a set of administrative, policing and military organisations headed and more or less well coordinated by an executive authority'.[43] This is 'an autonomous structure – a structure with a logic and interests of its own'. Mann refers to his own approach as 'Institutional statism'.[44] Despite the diversity of their viewpoints and theoretical differences, these writers have been dubbed 'organizational materialists'.[45] A fundamental thesis deriving from their work is that when pursuing political objectives, state managers are self-interested maximisers whose main interests is to enhance their own institutional power, prestige and wealth. Thus, 'organizational realists view states not only as decision-making organizations but also as autonomous

---

[38] Collins, Randall. *Weberian Sociological Theory*. Cambridge: Cambridge University Press, pp. 146–147.

[39] Michael, Mann. *The Sources of Social Power: Volume 1, A History of Power from the Beginning to AD 1760: V. 1.* 1st ed. Cambridge: Cambridge University Press, 1986; Mann, Michael. *The Sources of Social Power: Volume 2, the Rise of Classes and Nation-States, 1760–1914.* 2nd ed. Cambridge: Cambridge University Press, 2012.

[40] Poggi, Gianfranco. *The State, its Nature, Development and Prospects.* Stanford: Stanford University Press, 1990.

[41] Skocpol, Theda. *States and Social Revolutions.* Cambridge: Cambridge University Press, 1979; Evans, Peter, Dieter Rueschemeyer, Theda Skocpol. *Bringing the State Back In: Strategies of Analysis in Current Research.* Cambridge: Cambridge University Press, 1985.

[42] Tilly, Charles. *The Formation of National States in Western Europe.* Princeton, NJ: Princeton University Press, 1975; Tilly, Charles. *Coercion, Capital and European States, 990–1990.* Blackwell: Oxford, 1990.

[43] Skocpol, *States and Social Revolutions*, p. 27.

[44] Mann, *Social Sources Vol II*, p. 53.

[45] Barrow, Clyde. W. *Critical Theories of the State: Marxist, Post Marxist and Postmodernist.* Wisconson: University of Wisconsin Press, 1993.

organizational actors that must be considered real historical subjects in relation to social classes'.[46]

According to Bourdieu, Weber retains a 'physicalist' theory of the state. By contrast to 'physicalist' approaches that correlate domination largely to material or military forces, including the army or police force, Bourdieu – paradoxically drawing on Weber's other writings on domination and legitimation – argues that no power can be exercised only as naked power,[47]. Physicalist theories lack an explanation of how the social order is constituted in the first place, why the dominated submit so easily to their domination and overlook the fact that systems of domination based solely on force are fragile and easy to overthrow. Instead, symbolic forms need to be recognised for the central role that they play in state domination. This provides the basis for Bourdieu's definition of the state as a 'monopoly of legitimate physical and symbolic violence',[48] which he believes constitutes an essential corrective to Weber's restricted understanding. This definition is not proposed merely as a supplement to Weber's: rather, Bourdieu believes that his definition of the state underlies or furnishes the condition of possibility for Weber's focus on physical force. In addition to this truncated definition of the state Weber also fails to address in any satisfactory manner who possesses the monopoly of the monopoly of physical (and symbolic) violence and what interests its serves.[49]

DURKHEIM ON THE STATE

Writing in the aftermath and within the legacy of the French Revolution and the immediate political context of German victory in the Franco-Prussian War of 1870–1871 as well as in an intellectual context where French positivist philosophy of Saint-Simon and Comte is dominant, Durkheim, in his theory of the state, attempts to confront a number of political, social and ideological problems facing France. This includes the social and class conflicts between a republican tradition – for which he is an

---

[46] Ibid., 125.

[47] 'Domination, even when based on naked force, that of arms or money, always has a symbolic dimension'. Bourdieu, *Pascalian Meditations*, p. 172.

[48] Bourdieu, *Rethinking the State*, p. 3.

[49] Bourdieu, *On the State*, p. 125.

ideological spokesperson, a rising working class and a reactionary, conservative Catholic standpoint.

His theory of the state unfolds within his conception of a broader shift from mechanical to organic solidarity, from small-scale homogenous communities with low levels of social differentiation to large-scale differentiated modern industrial societies vividly outlined in his *The Division of Labour in Society* (1984).[50] For Durkheim, change is predominantly evolutionary not revolutionary taking place in the context of long-term processes of social development. The rise in social differentiation not only frees the individual increasingly from the *conscience collective*, eradicates regional differences and culture under the weight of industrialisation, but also facilitates the 'gradual aggregation' of minor societies and the emergence of secondary social groups subject to the one same political society.[51]

According to Durkheim, collective representations – be they myths, religion or morals – exist throughout society, yet they remain diffuse and endure on a semi-conscious or unconscious basis. The actions of individuals are unthinking, spontaneous and based on habit. By contrast, state representations and forms of thought are self-conscious, developed through clear and systematic reflection and provide the possibility of different deliberated forms of action: 'the state is a special organ whose responsibility it is to work out certain representations which hold good for the collectivity. These representations are distinguished from other collective representations by their higher degree of consciousness and reflection'.[52] Drawing on the analogy between the muscular system and the central nervous system, he argues that the principal function of the state is to think – the state is a 'social brain'. In this circumscribed view of

---

[50] Durkheim, Emile. *The Division of Labour in Society*. London: MacMillan, 1984.

[51] For Durkheim, the terms political society and state need to be kept separate: 'Since we need a word to indicate the particular group of officials entrusted with representing this authority, we are agreed to keep for this purpose the word "State"... But it is well to have separate words for existent things as different as the society and one of its organs, we apply the term "State" more especially to the agents of the sovereign authority, and political society to the complex group of which the state is the highest organ' Durkheim, Émile. *Professional Ethics and Civic Morals*. 2nd ed. New York: Taylor & Francis, 1992, pp. 47–48.

[52] Ibid., p. 50.

the state, other administrative bodies, including the executive, government or various bodies which carry out what are ordinarily perceived to be state actions, are excluded. The central role of the state is not action, but deliberation, or in constituting representations. Nevertheless, these representations have a practical rather than speculative aim. As an organ of moral regulation and discipline, guiding collective conduct, a fundamental aim or end of the state is to protect individual rights that have emerged historically in the transition from mechanical to organic solidarity. Here the cult and the dignity of the individual reigns, the individual constitutes an 'autonomous centre of activity'.[53] The state is therefore not antagonistic to the individual, as many political theorists from Locke to Mills have wrongly proclaimed, but a condition for the emergence of moral individualism: 'there is nothing negative in the part played by the State'.[54] It is 'only through the state that individualism is possible, although it cannot be the means of making it a reality...We might say the state is the prime mover. It is the State that has rescued the child from patriarchal domination and from family tyranny; it is the State that has freed the citizen from feudal groups and later from communal groups; it is the State that has liberated the craftsmen and his master from guild tyranny'.[55]

The state is above all an 'organ of social thought' elaborating definite representations for the collectivity and whose responsibility is to instill moral discipline. It both partially constitutes society's sentiments and ideals, the moral order, and reflects the universal interests of those over whom it governs by promoting moral individualism. The state implements the values of moral individualism in modern societies, replacing the Church – which had formerly played this role in traditional societies – as the primary institution for imposing and maintaining values.

Durkheim, like Bourdieu after him, tends to vacillate between a position that regards state thought as all pervasive and expanding throughout collective life – 'the State must therefore enter into their lives, it must supervise and keep a check on the way they operate and to do this it must spread its roots in all directions...it must be present

---

[53] Durkheim, *Professional Ethics*, p. 56.
[54] Ibid., p. 56.
[55] Ibid., p. 64.

in spheres of social life and make itself felt' – and a standpoint in which state thought and collective thought represent two different, though connected, forms of collective psychic life:

> The State, we said, is the organ of social thought. That does not mean that all social thought springs from the State. But there are two kinds. One comes from the collective mass of society and is diffused throughout the mass; it is made up of those sentiments, ideals, beliefs that the society has worked out collectively and with time, and that are strewn in the consciousness of each one. The other is worked out in the special organ called the state or government. The two are closely related. The vaguely diffused sentiments that float about the whole expanse of society affect the decisions made by the State, and conversely, those decisions made by the State, the ideas expounded in the Chamber, the speeches made there and the measures agreed upon by the ministeries, all have an echo in the whole of the society and modify the ideas strewn there.[56]

The State not only reflects the wishes of its members but leads them by instilling ideas and beliefs centred on the fostering of moral individualism, individual self-realisation and a form of social solidarity that underpins his vision of a liberal form of Republican – socialism. For Durkheim, it is both possible and necessary for individuals to give themselves to the state without becoming alienated and dominated by the state as an external, overwhelming and dominant power.

The shift from small-scale mechanical to large-scale organic society also engenders other changes. In organic societies, secondary groups based on local and professional interests – families, trades, clans, churches, towns, and associations, emerge. These groupings, however, should be hindered from becoming autonomous from society and thereby allowed to repress and monopolise individuals' personalities and freedoms 'and mould them at will'.[57] There must, therefore, exist above these secondary authorities, some overall authority. For Durkheim this is the state. It is the state which

---

[56] Ibid., p. 79. 'In fact, the State is nothing if not an organ an organ distinct from society. If the State is everywhere it is nowhere. The State comes into existence by a process of concentration that detaches a certain group of individuals from the mass. In that group the social thought is subjected to elaboration of a special kind and reaches a very high degree of clarity...'. Ibid., p. 82.

[57] Ibid., p. 62.

reminds these groups that they are a *part* and not the *whole*. Conversely, a dialectical relationship between the state and secondary and occupational groupings curbs state power checking the developmment of a rampant despotism.

As social life becomes more complex, so correspondingly does the nature of the state. This also explains why the state will continue to expand in the future. In a context of international competition in which states threaten one another, a primary duty of the state is to protect the collectivity and organise it accordingly. In such a scenario it may need to attack other states in order to defend itself. For Durkheim, what binds individuals to the state is a form of patriotism which confers responsibilities, duties and obligations on the individual on a national level, instilling national pride. However, under the weight of increasing division of labour within the international order, this is increasingly giving way to a form of world patriotism or cosmopolitanism where humanity in its entirety is organised as society.

In his ruminations on the state the particular form taken by states in relation to citizens – as an aristocracy, monarchy or democracy tends to remain of secondary importance. Aristocratic or monarchical constitutions are only differentiated by matters of degree. It is the distinction between the consciousness of a clear reflective state and the nameless and indistinct representations of the unthinking mass that matters and it is this that defines democracy.

> To sum up, there is not, strictly speaking, any inherent difference between the various forms of government; but they all lie intermediate between two contrasting schemes. At one extreme, the government consciousness is as isolated as possible from the rest of society and has a minimum range ... The closer communication becomes between the government consciousness and the rest of society, and the more this consciousness expands and the more things it takes in, the democratic the character of society will be. The concept of democracy is best seen in the extension of this consciousness to its maximum and it is this process that determines the communication.[58]

According to Durkheim, there has been an increasing flow of ideas over time from the state to the wider society so that the state no longer remains

---

[58] Ibid., p. 84.

withdrawn but penetrates into the deeper layers of society, ideas, which in turn flow back into the state. The state, which in democratic societies is more malleable and flexible, has now a wider influence while the sphere of a clear, reflective consciousness has expanded throughout the population rendering visible but also modifying habitual habits. A democratic society, he argues, is a reflexive society conscious of itself, like the brain that thinks as opposed to the body that acts automatically. Political parties, parliament and the franchise, therefore, play a less important role in his analysis than an exclusive focus on the interchange of ideas and sentiments between the state and population.

Although Bourdieu, in *On the State* for example, engages with both the work of Marx and Weber, albeit briefly, he has surprisingly little to say about Durkheim's theory with the exception of seeing Durkheim as a representative of state thought more generally: 'The state involves objectification and all the techniques of objectification. It deals with social facts as things, with men as things – it is Durkeimian *avant la letter*. That is why Durkheim's theory of the state was the internalized state. A state functionary who did not see himself as a state functionary, he was in the state like a fish in water; he had an objectivist theory of the social world, which is the implicit perception that the state has of its subjects'.[59] This limited and clipped reflection is odd given that his own theory of the state can in some ways be read as a synthesis of the Weberian with the Durkheimian view of the state, or more specifically a reinterpretation of Weber's theory of the state, domination and legitimation filtered through a Durkheimian state optic.

MODERN THEORIES OF THE STATE

Although Bourdieu argues he is drawing upon specific and indispensable themes in the writings of all three classical theorists – Marx's analysis of primitive accumulation; Weber's concept of legitimation, monopolisation of physical force and rationalisation; and Durkheim's discussion of the social division of labour and the social nature of the categories[60] – he accepts none of their writings on the state, taken either singularly or collectively, criticising all three. In *On the State*, however, he also engages

[59] Bourdieu, *On the State*, p. 214.
[60] Ibid., pp. 70–71.

with a number of modern interpretations of the state which he selectively uses as a sounding board against which he develops his own view of a specific state logic. Three of the most significant – the work of Elias, Tilly and Corrigan and Sayer – will be reviewed here.

ELIAS AND THE STATE

Within the context of a figurational analysis of the power dynamics characterising social relations and processes within a long-term framework, Elias in *The Civilising Process* draws on Marx, Mannheim, Weber, Simmel and Freud to offer an investigation of psychological and behavioural transformations among the secular upper classes in the West. These, Elias showed, were integrally tied to processes of internal pacification and state formation. Asking how it was that certain classes in the developing nation-states of Western Europe came to think of themselves as 'civilized' and how this became generalised as a badge of Western superiority over non-western cultures, Elias charted long-term transformations in manners, behavioural codes and thresholds of repugnance concerning bodily functions, all of which involved an internalisation of social restraints. He then traced the establishment of a characteristic habitus, involving increasing superego restraints over affective impulses and drives (including violent behaviour), as a compelling aspect of court society, arguing that upper-class manners and affective sensibility, through processes of distinction and imitation, had become generalised as examples of polite behaviour and gradually diffused through other strata. This blind and unplanned – but nevertheless structured and directional – transformation of manners was the primary subject of Volume I of *The Civilising Process*. In Volume II, he turned to state formation and the 'sociogenesis' of the absolutist states and showed how the internalisation of restraints and the resulting transformation in behavioural codes were intimately connected with transformations in the division of labour, demographic shifts, societal pacification, urbanisation and the growth of trade and a money economy. The expansion of the urban money economy facilitated, but also critically depended upon, the power and the monopoly of violence achieved by the central state authority. For Elias, the state is defined in terms of its twin monopoly of violence and taxation; they form two sides of the same coin. In discussing state formation, Elias discusses the shift in power from private monopoly of the king to a public monopoly of a bureaucratic state. Greater access to economic circuits gave access to greater military resources relative to the landed warlord-nobility, whose principal source of economic and military power was control over finite and depreciating land assets. This shifting power ratio transformed a formerly independent warrior class into an increasingly dependent upper class of courtiers. Greater pacification facilitated trade and economic growth, which in turn underwrote the economic and military power of the central authority and led to growing power for the middle classes. When declining aristocratic power and increasing middle-class power were approximately equal, monarchs were able to lay claim to 'absolute power'. In their newly pacified domains, and particularly within the court, these developments systematically rewarded more restrained patterns of behaviour. External restraints, associated with the authority relations of state formation, were gradually and increasingly internalised as self-restraints, resulting in a characteristic shift in habitus and personality structure.

Bourdieu criticizes Elias in three major respects.[61] First, he argues that Elias simply provides a Weberian 'physicalist theory' of the state that ignores the symbolic dimension necessary for maintaining state legitimacy and power.[62] Second, he argues that Elias's definition of the monopoly mechanism is tautological since it ignores the means or assets available to a king which had led to his triumph in the competition with his rivals: that is 'what he [Norbert Elias] calls the "law of monopoly", a solution that I shall not discuss in detail here but which seems to me to be essentially verbal and almost tautological'.[63] Third, Elias, Like Weber, ignores the fact that a small group of individuals – the state nobility – secures a monopoly over the monopoly. Counterbalancing these criticisms,

---

[61] One of these is idiosyncratic: 'I am a strong defender of Elias's ideas, but I begin to be somewhat vexed by the fact that he enjoys a kind of sacralization today'. Bourdieu, *On the State*, p. 199.

[62] The word "legitimate", if you take it quite seriously, is enough to evoke the symbolic dimension of this violence, since the idea of legitimacy includes the idea of recognition. Despite everything, however, Weber did not develop this aspect of the state in his theory very strongly; with Elias, this aspect – disappears almost completely. That is the main criticism I make of his model. Elias, in fact, lets the symbolic dimension of state power disappear, and essentially retains the constitution of a double monopoly, that of physical violence and that of taxation Bourdieu, *On the State*, p. 128.

[63] Bourdieu, *From the King's House*, p. 33.

Bourdieu adds: 'Where I do see Elias as truly innovative, and I will draw on this to develop the genetic theory of the state, is in the elements of the analysis he makes of the transition from a private monopoly (what I call the dynastic state) to the public monopoly of the state'.[64] Although he explicitly acknowledges using Elias's genetic theory of the state and his transition from the dynastic state to the bureaucratic state, it is clear that he actually draws on much more. This includes: (i) Elias's view that the state 'is a legitimate protection racket'; (ii) that the state was Janus-faced, so that together with monopolisation of the means of violence and taxation there comes increasing peace, even for the most disadvantaged groups; (iii) processes of differentiation, lengthening chains of dependence and interdependence lead to relations of asymmetrical dependency and legitimation; (iv) that the king operates a policy of divide and conquer – what Elias calls the 'royal mechanism'; (v) that the more power becomes concentrated, the more difficult it becomes for the ruler to control it, and his dependency on others increases; (vi) that taxes are bound up in a reciprocal virtuous cycle with warfare.[65]

Bourdieu's criticisms of Elias are of a mixed nature. Some penetrating, others miss the mark completely.[66]

CHARLES TILLY

In *Capital, Coercion and European States AD990–1992*, Tilly analyses a diversity of national state modalities including the English, French, Russian, Swedish and Dutch forms. On the basis of their divergences and overlaps, he constructs his own model. In a capacious definition foregrounding

---

[64] Bourdieu, *On the State*, p. 128.

[65] More generally, there are numerous other parallels in their work, both use the notion of habitus and field, seek to transcend the agency-structure divide, and both see state formation as inextricably tied to changes in personality structure and both, following Durkheim, argue that as societies advance they differentiate into separate spheres. They also share a broadly similar world-social democratic view. Though some of the differences in terms of physical violence and symbolic violence can also be accounted for by the paradigmatic crises situations they both respond to – the aftermath of the violence of the First World War and Algeria respectively.

[66] These are reviewed in Loyal, Steven. 'Bourdieu's theory of the state: an Eliasian Critique' in *Human Figurations. Vol 5: 2. 2016*

coercion and territory, he defines states as 'coercion-wielding organizations that are distinct from households and kinship groups and exercise clear priorities in some respects over all other organizations within substantial territories'.[67] The system of national states that currently predominates over the planet emerged in Europe after AD 990. For Tilly this poses a critical double question: 'What accounts for the great variation over time and space in the kinds of states that have prevailed in Europe since AD 990, and why did European states eventually converge on different variants of the national state'?[68] In this diversity, France and England indicate just one path in national state formation among others. Drawing on Rokkan, Barrington-Moore and Mumford, his own model places the organisation of coercion and preparation for war central to state analysis. Relations among states, especially through war and its preparation, permeated the entire process of state formation. Within the major changes that took place in the relationship between warfare and state organisation in the 1000 years between 990AD and 1990 four significant phases can be delimited: patrimonialism which existed up to the 15th century; a phase of brokerage between 1400 and 1700; a phase of nationalisation between 1700 and 1850; and a final stage of specialisation from the mid-19th century to the immediate past.

According to Tilly, the divergent histories of state-formation are a result of the varying combinations of concentrated capital, concentrated coercion, preparation for war, and position within the international state system. The processes that accumulate and concentrate capital also produce cities, which, as forms of regional economy, constitute favoured sites for capitalists, as well as organisational forces in their own right. Coercion, which also concentrates, includes the concerted application of action that commonly causes loss or damage to the persons or possessions of individuals or groups. When accumulation and concentration grow simultaneously, they produce states. It is the interactive relation between coercion, centred on states, and capital, focused on cities, that is between exploitation and domination, which is central. Tilly identifies three different types of state that have proliferated in Europe since AD 990. These are tribute-taking empires mainly operating under conditions of low accumulation and high concentration of coercion; systems of fragmented

---

[67] Tilly, *Capital, Coercion*, p. 1.

[68] Ibid., p. 5.

sovereignty such as city-states with high accumulations and low concentrations of coercion; and national states with high accumulation and high concentration of coercion. It is the preparation for war mixed with these other factors of capital and coercive concentration which explains different state formation

Given the diversity of capital and coercion combinations, Tilly suggests three major forms which structured different paths to state formation and which represented contrasting conditions of life; capital-intensive; coercion-intensive; and a capitalised–coercion path. When capital accumulation was high but coercive authority low or diffuse, city-states, city empires and urban federations such as Genoa, Venice and the Dutch Republic emerged. Where capital was low or diffuse and coercion high, rulers depended on the use of coercion to force their own population and others they conquered to build massive structures of extraction, with Russia and Brandenburg serving as exemplars. In areas where capital accumulation and coercion were balanced, or formed an intermediate mode between these two aforementioned extremes, as in England and France, large standing armies would usually emerge as holders of capital and coercion interacted in terms of relative equality. Gradually, over a period of time, the superiority of capital-coercive states in waging war with other states led to the formation of national states as a predominant social form:

> From the seventeenth century onward the capitalized coercion form proved more effective in war, and therefore provided a compelling model for states that had originated in other combinations of coercion and capital. From the nineteenth century to the recent past, furthermore, all European states involved themselves much more heavily than before in building social infrastructure, in providing services, in regulating economic activity, in controlling population movements, and in assuring citizens' welfare; all these activities began as by products of rulers' efforts to acquire revenues and compliance from their subject populations, but took on lives and rationales of their own.[69]

The variation in the accumulation and concentration of capital explains the emergence of different state forms while the waging of war explains the

---

[69] Ibid., p. 31.

move towards national state formation. Even after convergence, however, states retained some of their original features.

For Bourdieu, there are many significant parallels between Tilly and Weber and Elias's work. Like Weber and Elias, whose model Tilly advances upon, the symbolic dimension of state domination remains absent and, like both, he remains trapped in an economism or economic logic which ignores the development of a unique, irreducible state logic. By contrast specifically to Elias, however, Tilly fails to engage with the move from a private to a public monopoly or to analyse how chains of interdependence are created. Nevertheless, Bourdieu argues: 'one of the major results of Tilly's analysis is to show why England and France are particular cases that I can use for my model'.[70]

CORRIGAN AND SAYER

Finally, we can briefly review Bourdieu's discussion of Corrigan & Sayer's interpretation of the nature of the state contained in *The Great Arch: State Formation as Cultural Revolution*. This work closely resembles Bourdieu's own given the prominent role accorded to Durkheim's theory of the state as a moral authority. Drawing on Marx's theory of class, Weber's analysis of authority and legitimation, Durkheim's emphasis on moral discipline and Abram's (1988) discussion of the state as politically organised subjection, they examine the long timeframe within which the bourgeois revolution in England unfolded between the 11th and 19th century and its attendant peculiarities.

State formation, they argue, needs to be understood as a cultural revolution in the making of a bourgeois civilisation. Unlike Bourdieu, Corrigan and Sayer focus markedly on the connection between state formation and the rise of modern capitalism. They propose an approach in which the meaning of state activities, routines and rituals is central to regulating social identities and subjectivities. The state, as a Durkheimian organ of moral discipline, draws upon a wider *conscience collective* – as consciousness and conscience – which it regulates. State formation is coextensive with 'moral regulation'. The collective representations, ways in which individuals are represented to themselves and

---

[70] Bourdieu, *On the State*, p. 135.

the parameters through which they can identify, are simultaneously descriptive and moral:

> The repertoire of activities and institutions usually defined as 'the State' are cultural forms central to bourgeois civilization: states, if the pun be forgiven, state . . . They define, in great detail, acceptable forms and images of social activity and individual and collective identity; they regulate, in empirically specifiable ways, much – very much, by the twentieth century – of social life. Indeed, in this sense "the state" never stops talking . . . Out of the vast range of human social capacities – possible ways in which social life could be lived- state activities more or less forcibly "encourage" some while suppressing, marginalizing, eroding, undermining others. Schooling for instance comes to stand for education, policing for order, voting for political participation. Fundamental social classifications, like age and gender, are enshrined in law, embedded in institutions, routinized in administrative procedures and symbolized in rituals of state. Certain forms of activity are given the seal of approval, others are situated beyond the pale. This has cumulative, and enormous, cultural consequences; consequences for how people identify (in many cases, have to identify) themselves and their "place" in the world.[71]

As well as regulating subjectivities and organizing time and space, the class, ethnic and gendered aspect of state formation forms a central focus of their work. The forms of cultural relations which states regulate have multiple effects on a population differentiated according to class, gender, ethnicity, age, religion, occupation and locality. State agencies, however, attempt to provide a singular expression to what are fragmented and multifaceted experiences. The *collective conscience* the state regulates is always that of a dominant class, gender and ethnicity idealising its conditions of rule as rules of individual conduct. State formation can therefore be seen differently from above and from below. It has a totalising aspect by representing peoples as members of what Marx in the *German Ideology* calls an 'illusory community', the nation, which becomes their central mode of identification and loyalty. Nationality, in turn, allows a categorisation of outsiders and others. States also individualise individuals: people are registered as citizens, voters, parents, homeowners. In both instances, alternative forms of collective class and individual identification are denied legitimacy. Not only do states oppress collectivities, but they also empower individuals, in 'differentiated

---

[71] Corrigan and Sayer, *The Great Arch*, pp. 3–4.

and differentiating ways – husbands against wives, gentlemen against labourers, Englishmen against Irish, Anglicans against Catholics –as agents in the social arena which state regulation seeks to concert'.[72]

Recognising the degree of mutuality between consensus and coercion, they posit that although violence (including that of the armies, prisons, workhouses) underpins both *habitus* and consent, it has to be connected to ideological processes. 'The state is not only external and objective but, internal and subjective': 'it works through us. It works above all through the myriad ways it collectively and individually (mis) represents us and variously "encourages", cajoles and in the final analysis forces us to (mis) represent ourselves. Over the centuries the compass of this regulation has ever widened, and such regulation is (partly) constitutive of "available" modes of being human'.[73] In addition, they argue that making this *conscience collective* is always an accomplishment, a struggle against other moralities and other ways of seeing, which express 'the historical experiences of the dominated' and because 'society is not factually a unity these can never be fully erased'.[74]

The state, they add, is not a thing to be captured or smashed or some impersonal power like Hobbes's Mortall God. Following Abrams – who argued that sociologists often attribute the idea of the state too much coherence and concreteness – Corrigan and Sayer believe that the state needs to be seen as a 'collective misrepresentation of capitalist society'.

The focus on long-term processes of struggle and alternative ways of seeing this struggle lead them to assert that forcing what is called the 'English revolution' into the conceptual straight-jacket of a bourgeois revolution, is highly problematic. The idea of a rupture in which political power changes hand 'seriously obscures, and massively simplifies, the complex and protracted history of state formation and transformations through which capitalists classes did come finally to achieve political dominance in England'.[75]

Bourdieu shares Corrigan and Sayers attempts to move away from Marxist-functionalist analyses of the state, and especially the Leninist

---

[72] Corrigan & Sayer, p. 214.

[73] Corrigan and Sayer, *The Great Arch*, p. 180.

[74] Ibid., p. 6.

[75] Ibid., p. 85.

view, by examining the state instead as a set of cultural forms that regulates subjectivities and 'domesticates the dominated'. He also concurs in their use of Marx, Weber and Durkheim: 'They are interesting because they juggle between Marx, Durkheim and Weber – as I believe you have to in order to understand state questions'. He adds: 'If I agree with them completely on this, it is because they use Durkheim to give meaning to a question of Weber, and at the same time do not forget Marx, they do not forget that this organ of moral discipline is not just in the service of anyone, but rather serves the dominant'.[76] He also extends and modifies their discussion on the English revolution – that is, that there was no contradiction between the fact that the English did not have a French style Revolution but nevertheless underwent an industrial revolution. This applies equally to the notion of a French revolution 'which is a false revolution'. The fact that *the noblesse de robe* continued in power both prior to and after what are perceived as drastic political changes having taken place questions the idea of any revolutionary break. The French model of revolution, which has served as a yardstick for all forms of revolutionary break, has 'generated heaps of false questions all over the world'. Although Bourdieu does not say as much, such an evolutionary standpoint has a basis both in Durkheim's view of society as well as in Hegel, who believed that the idea of the French revolution as a break with a Medieval past 'was one of the silliest of notions'.[77]

Despite the profound and unquestionable similarities between their perspectives on the state, Bourdieu chastises Corrigan and Sayer 'as sociologists doing history', whose work he believes is theoretically confusing and unclear, especially since they lack the concepts of symbolic power or symbolic violence. This means they are unable to *explain* 'the voluntary submission, voluntary dependence, that the state obtains, this kind of submission that escapes the alternative between coercion and freely chosen submission'.[78]

Despite his claim to have surmounted many of the antinomies pervading their analysis, there is one respect in which their work surpasses his, and this is their stronger focus on both the class and the gendered

---

[76] *On the State*, p. 141.

[77] Cited in Beiser, Frederick. *Hegel*, London: Routledge, 2005. p. 251.

[78] *On the State*, p. 146.

dimension of the state. We shall discuss the omission of the class dimension of the state in chapter 7. But it is of some significance that the gendered aspect of the state remains absent not only from Bourdieu's understanding but also from many of the state theorists he selectively reviews.

Having provided a schematic overview of the different classical and modern theories of the state, we are now in a improved position to examine Bourdieu's theory of the state in the next chapter.

CHAPTER 4

Bourdieu's Theory of the State

Abstract This chapter outlines Bourdieu's theory of the state as a monopoly of physical and symbolic violence. It examines Bourdieu's view that
the state exists both outside and within social actors. It highlights the
state's power of naming, authority and processes of delegation through
acts of state.

Keywords Symbolic capital · Legitimation · Acts of state · Symbolic bank
of credit

THE STATE AS A MONOPOLY OF PHYSICAL AND SYMBOLIC VIOLENCE

The state, Bourdieu tells us, is the sector of the field of power, or bureaucratic field, which is defined by a possession of the monopoly of legitimate
physical *and* symbolic violence: 'the state is an X (to be determined) which
successfully claims the monopoly of the legitimate use of physical and
symbolic violence over a definite territory and over the totality of the
corresponding population'.[1]

Although Weber is clearly present in this definition, it is from Durkheim,
and to a lesser extent, Cassirer, and structuralism that his theory draws

---

[1] Bourdieu, *Rethinking the State*, p. 3.

its originality. This specifically concerns a cluster of concepts relating to symbolic forms – symbolic capital, symbolic power and symbolic violence. Although Bourdieu talks about a dual monopoly of legitimate physical and symbolic violence, it is the latter that is prioritised in his work and, as we shall see, the former, force and violence, remains largely absent or peripheral in his discussion. For Bourdieu, the monopolisation of symbolic violence is a *condition* for the exercise of a monopoly of physical violence. His definition of the state therefore underlies Weber's restricted focus on physical force. By contrast to 'physicalist' approaches (which in addition to Weber also include Marx and others, such as Elias and Tilly) that correlate domination largely to material or military forces, including the army or police force, Bourdieu, following Pascal (and paradoxically other aspects of the work of Weber concerned with legitimation)[2] asserts that no power can be exercised only as naked power:

> Force acts directly, by physical constraint, but also through the representation that those subject to it have of this force; the most brutal and violent force obtains a form of recognition that goes beyond mere submission to its physical effect...there is no physical effect in the social world that is not accompanied by a symbolic effect...the strange logic of human action means that brute force is never only brute force: it exerts a form of seduction, persuasion, which bears on the fact that it manages to obtain a certain form of recognition.[3]

Here two points are stressed. First, all physical violence also contains a symbolic dimension. The material/physical and ideal and symbolic aspects of force cannot be separated, and in fact the latter has priority. Second, the two processes of violence only make sense when they are recognised by a collectivity of agents with specific dispositions or a specific habitus. By contrast, physicalist theories lack an explanation of how the social order is

---

[2] Thus, whilst discussing charisma and legitimation Weber discusses: 'the need of social strata, privileged through existing political, social and economic orders, to have their social and economic positions 'legitimized'. They wish to see their positions transformed from purely factual power relations into a cosmos of acquired rights, and to know they are thus sanctified', Weber, Max. 'The Meaning of Discipline' in Hans Gerth and Charles Wright Mills (eds) *From Max Weber: Essays in Sociology*, London: Routledge: 2009, p. 262.

[3] *On the State*, p. 192.

constituted in the first place and why the dominated submit so easily to state domination. They overlook the fact that modes of domination deriving exclusively from force are amenable to being deposed. The central questions, for Bourdieu, then turn on *state legitimation* in the maintenance of social order, of sustaining authority and acquiring consent, a problem addressed not only by Weber and Pascal but also by philosophers including Spinoza and Hume.

The operation of symbolic forms and symbolic power in reproducing the social order entails the imposition, through struggles and confrontations, of the social visions of dominant social groups upon the competing social viewpoints of the social world held by dominated groups. Systems of meaning, classification and signification are integrally involved in maintaining social domination by masking the arbitrary nature of the domination so that it is (mis)recognised by the dominated. As well as drawing on Cassirer theories of symbolic forms as structuring structures, and structuralism's emphasis on the coherence of symbolic systems as structured structures, Bourdieu draws on the distinction that Durkheim makes in *The Elementary forms of Religious Life*[4] between logical and moral conformity. As we noted earlier, the former refers to the 'homogenous conception of time, space, number and cause, one which makes it possible for different intellects to reach agreement'[5]; this is the precondition of moral integration in which there is a consensus on the values and moral meaning of the world.

The state is the foundation of logical and moral conformity of the social world, creating both sense and consensus. It constitutes the hidden principle of orthodoxy that becomes manifest in social and public order. It is through the immediate agreement of people with similar categories of thought and perception, generated by the state, and inscribed in things

---

[4] Durkheim, Émile. 1912. *The Elementary Forms of Religious Life: Newly Translated by Karen E. Fields.* New York: Simon & Schuster, 1996.

[5] Echoing Husserl, it is only through possessing shared logical categories that we can have dissensus and conflict: 'The state is that which founds the logical conformity of the social world, and in this way, the fundamental consensus on the meaning of the social world that is the very precondition of conflict over the social world. In other words for conflict to be possible, a kind of agreement is needed on the grounds of disagreement and on their modes of expression. *On the State*. p. 4.

in the social world, that state power as symbolic power creates belief, obedience and a consensus in the dominated:

> the state establishes and inculcates common forms and categories of perception and appreciation, social frameworks of perceptions, of understanding or of memory, in short state forms of classification. It thereby creates the conditions for a kind of immediate orchestration of habituses which is itself the foundation of a consensus over this set of shared evidences constitutive of (national) common sense.[6]

Through the respect they show towards the social world, all social agents in society, though to differing degrees, unwittingly reproduce the social order. The deference paid to officials, but more specifically through them as representatives of the state order, illustrates a process that Spinoza terms *'obsequium'*. This deference is not gained through a conscious duping, or from acquiring the consent of individuals to a ruling class ideology as Marxists posit, but through the unconscious agreement between state categories and the social order, mental structures and social structures. That is, it is obtained through classifications and the mechanism of belief inscribed in the body, as embodied categories, that correspond to the hierarchical structure of the social world. The concept of *doxa*, derived from Husserl's notion of *urdoxa*, though with roots in Plato, does not simply concern legitimisation or a 'propaganda action' as ideology does for Marxists, rather it is about the *constitutive* aspect of discourse in social life. Doxa does not *rationalise* social reality but *makes* it.

The cognitive structures individuals internalise and apply to the social world, which are both descriptive and evaluative, are constituted by the state and operate 'through belief and the pre-agreement of the body and the mind with the world':

> What is internalized, in my view are principles of vision and division of the world, which being in agreement with the objective structures of the world, create a sort of infra-conscious fit with the structures within which individuals evolve. So that domination operates through belief, through a doxic relation to structures. It appears as a natural order. It is

---

[6] Bourdieu, *Rethinking*, p. 13.

this infra- conscious complicity between habitus and field which, in many universes, explains the submission of the dominated (which has nothing to do with love of power or of the censor, as a superficial usage of psychoanalysis might suggest). Nor has it to do with a guilt-ridden surrender, extorted through cowardice or bad faith. It results rather from the agreement that obtains between conditions of existence and the dispositions that these conditions have produced.[7]

This pre-reflexive adhesion to the social order means that the state with its ability to impose universal principles of vision and division and classification, or *nomos*, generates a belief effect, a 'magical effect', in which the majority of the population obeys or follows its rules and orders, without the state necessarily having to exercise any physical coercion or stipulate any requests or orders. This increased emphasis on symbolic forms and culture in maintaining and reproducing the social order does not, Bourdieu believes, mean relapsing into an idealism; rather it entails what he calls an 'expanded materialism', or a 'materialist theory of the symbolic', where symbolic and material forms of domination coexist. His work on the state and state formation, therefore, attempts to provide an analysis of the initial accumulation of symbolic forms – which we shall examine in Chapter 6 – as part of an expanded materialism:

> I believe that the initial accumulation . . . the whole of my work is intended to produce a materialist theory of the symbolic, which is traditionally opposed to the material. Impoverished materialist traditions that do not leave space for the symbolic have a hard time accounting for this kind of generalized obedience without appealing to coercion, and moreover, they cannot understand the phenomenon of initial accumulation . . . I believe the primary form of accumulation takes place on the symbolic level. There are people who got themselves obeyed, respected because they are literate, religious, holy, handsome . . . in other words for heaps of reasons that materialism, in the ordinary sense, does not know what to do with.[8]

---

[7] Wacquant, Loic. 'From Ruling Class to Field of Power: An Interview with Pierre Bourdieu on La Noblesse d'Etat' *Theory, Culture and Society*, 10. 1993, pp. 34–35.
[8] Bourdieu, *On the State*, pp. 166–167.

As he also notes elsewhere, relations of communication are not wholly dissimilar from relations of force.[9]

In earlier, less differentiated, societies, the social principles of vision and division were based upon the opposition between masculine and feminine, and inscribed on bodies and minds through 'rites of institution',[10] which demarcate those who have undergone a rite from those who have not, and then subsequently by religion in the medieval world. In modern societies, it is the state, particularly through the school system, which is an 'immense rite of institution', that creates and inscribes *national* social divisions and hierarchies in people's mental structures: creating a social consensus and societal common sense. And it is for this reason that Bourdieu has written so extensively over the years on the role of the school system. Although the school may be seen as an institution of integration, providing all with the instruments of citizenship and economic access, something Bourdieu only mentions in his later writings whilst defending state intervention, it is simultaneously, if not primarily, the part of the state that by inculcating evaluative binary categories, produces principles of hierarchisation as well as 'national' forms of culture through an imposition of a cultural arbitrary. As we shall see in Chapter 5, in addition to this general role, the *Grand écoles* in France have a specific role in providing and producing a state nobility – personnel fulfilling the state's most important functions.

The State Exists Outside of *and* Within Individuals

The state, for Bourdieu, is not a monolithic, abstract, detached entity engaged in large-scale substantial acts as is commonly assumed – passing legislation, governing or producing legitimising discourses to serve dominant

---

[9] Bourdieu states: 'Relations of force are inseparable from relations of meaning and communication, the dominated are also people who know and acknowledge . . . The act of obedience presupposes an act of knowledge, which is at the same time an act of acknowledgement . . . the person who submits, who obeys, bends to an order or discipline, performs a cognitive action . . . Acts of submission and obedience are cognitive acts, and as such they bring into play cognitive structures, categories of perception, patterns of perception, principles of vision and division, a whole series of things that the neo-Kantian tradition emphasizes'. *On The State*, p. 164.

[10] Bourdieu, Pierre. 'Rites of Institution' in *Language and Symbolic Power*, Cambridge: Polity, pp. 117–126.

class interests. Rather more prosaically, and simultaneously more pro-foundly, the state operates in and through us. State thinking penetrates the minutest aspects of our everyday lives from filling in a bureaucratic form, carrying an identity card, signing a birth certificate, to shaping our day-to-day thinking and thought: it is the public at the heart of what we consider to be eminently private: 'the state structures the social order itself – timetables, budget periods, calendars, our whole social life is structured by the state – and, by the same token, so is our thought'.[11] The categories we work and live with, the practices we label, how we perceive and evaluate social processes are all effects of state thinking and categories. Things which appear trivial or mundane, such as arguing over spelling or following rituals and festive holidays, are in fact effects of state power revealing how the state structures our social temporality. Through its provision of a state instituted calendar, public temporal reference points for the seasons, the regulation of clock time, the synchronisation of activities, our temporal order is shaped by the state as well as our collective memory. Since ways of thinking, and the categories we use become deeply ingrained and instilled in our unconscious, they come to shape our social identities and modes of identification. Hence, though they appear *prima facie* as trivial, polemics concerning spelling reform for instance, a practice that is deeply embedded in our habitus, can take on a huge significance for the identity and vested interests of those involved.

> It [the state –SL] exists objectively in the form of grammar, the form of the dictionary, the form of the rules of spelling, government recommendations, the form of teachers of grammar text books of spelling, etc. and it exists in mental structures in the form of dispositions to write in the correct, that is corrected manner … What is important is doxic adherence to the necessity of orthography. The state can simultaneously ensure that there are teachers in spelling, and that there are people ready to die for correct spelling.[12]

For Bourdieu, then, the state is everywhere exercising an unconscious effect of symbolic imposition: objectively in things, the division in disciplines,

---

[11] Bourdieu, *On the State*, p. 183.

[12] Ibid., p. 121.

age-groups, official statistics, census categories, the curriculum, in national borders; and in mental structures, with the dispositions to classify and act in certain ways. The fact we speak a shared language within borders, follow the rules of grammar, heed government recommendations – processes that are taken for granted and naturalised through *doxa* – are an outcome of state effects.

In one summary of the state, Bourdieu argues that the state accomplishes three functions through its official institutional discourse: conferring social identity through acts of nomination; directing people's action and behaviour; and rationalising social processes and producing common sense. All three functions presuppose that it has the authority and the legitimate point of view to do so:

> firstly; it performs a diagnostic function, that is, an act of cognition which enforces recognition and which quite often tends to affirm what a person or a thing is and what it is universally, for every possible person, and thus objectively. It is an almost divine discourse, which assigns to every one an identity. In the second place, the administrative discourse, via directives, orders, prescriptions, etc., it says what people have to do, given what they are. Thirdly, it says what people really have done, as in authorised accounts such as police reports. In each case, it imposes a point of view, that of the institution, especially via questionnaires, official norms. This point of view is set up as a legitimate point of view, that is, as a point of view which everyone has to recognise at least within the limits of a given society. The representative of the state is the repository of common sense.[13]

The state not only contributes to the reproduction of the symbolic and social order but also makes it difficult to stand outside of that order. That is, individuals argue using its ideas and concepts but not over them, they become in Aristotle's term 'commonplaces'.[14] Consequently, individuals participate in what Marx calls an 'illusory community' within which they recognise the same universal principles.

[13] Bourdieu, *In Other Words*, p. 136.

[14] Bourdieu, Pierre. *Acts of Resistance: Against the Tyranny of the Market.* New York: The New Press, 1999, p. 8.

The State and Sociology

Given its ubiquitous but unconscious presence, the nature of the state constitutes one the most difficult question facing sociologists. This is in a two-fold sense since not only are state symbolic systems twice inscribed – in people's habitus, their categories of perception and classification *and* in the objective social world in things – which make a large number of practices and institutions appear natural and self-evident and encourage *doxic* adherence, but also because, as Durkheim recognised, there exists unconscious 'profound links', between sociology and the state. Here social problems become sociological problems: 'sociology' – and thus sociologists – are integrally connected to the state and that, consequently, 'thought on the state (*pensée de l'État*) is always liable to be state thought (*pensée d'État*)'.[15] 'If we are all', Bourdieu asks, using Thomas Bernard's words, 'servants of the state', how do we avoid thinking about the state without employing state thinking?: 'To endeavour to think the state is to take the risk of thinking over (or being taken over by) a thought of the state, i.e. of applying to the state categories of thought produced and guaranteed by the state and hence to misrecognize its most profound truth'.[16] Here, issues of reflexivity and misrecognition become central foci for sociologists as does the imperative to challenge the state's monopoly of the legitimate representation of the social world. If the state is a *meta* power as we shall see, then it is incumbent upon sociology, as part of a struggle over the field of representation of knowledge, to be '*meta-meta*' in questioning state constituted pre-notions.

The State as a Self-fulfilling Prophecy

Given the immense power of state thought to deceive us, sociologists (in addition to everyday actors) are often misled by what the state is and how it operates. The state is not what we think it is, but rather a collective illusion, a theological reality, like Durkheim's analysis of religion, created

---

[15] Wacquant, Loic. 'From Ruling Class to Field of Power', p. 40. He adds: 'When you read the texts that Durkheim has produced on the state, you cannot shake off the strong impression that it is the state that is thinking itself through the state thinker, the civil servant sociologist (*sociologue-functionnaire*)' Ibid.

[16] Bourdieu et al., *The Craft*, p. 1.

by our very understanding of it and belief in its existence. It is a product of our collective misrecognition which is experienced through its effects:

> The state is a well-founded illusion, this place that exists essentially because people believe that it exists. This illusory reality, collectively validated by consensus, is the site that you are headed towards when you go backward from a certain number of phenomena – educational qualifications, professional qualifications or calendar. Proceeding step by step, you arrive at a site that is the foundation of all this. This mysterious reality exists through its effects and through the collective belief in its existence which lies at the origin of these effects.[17]

The state exists in a specific way because people believe it exists in that way. It is real because people believe it is real. In effect, the state is a self-fulfilling prophecy. As a result of internalising state thinking, the state is reified and collectively misrecognised as an actual, substantial unified entity, an argument echoing Abrams's assertion that the state, as an ideological effect, appears as an organised, centralised object in people's perceptions.[18] Equally, for Bourdieu, the state is not akin to an object, it is not a bloc but a field of forces, a sector of the field of power which may be called the 'administrative' field, 'bureaucratic field' or 'field of public office'. As we shall see later, the notion of a reified state is a 'legal fiction' consisting of words and modes of organisation created by lawyers from the 12th century and later by theorists such as Bodin, in the 16th and 17th centuries, who through their performative discourse, which is misrecognized as straightforward description, recursively produce the very object they are talking about:

> the state is to a large extent the product of theorists. When they take the writings of Naude on the coup d'etat or Loyseau on the state, or the writings of all those lawyers in the sixteenth and seventeenth centuries who produced theories of the state, certain philosophers treat them like colleagues whose theories they are discussing, forgetting that these colleagues produced the very object they are reflecting on.[19]

---

[17] *On the State*, p. 10.

[18] Abrams, 'Notes on the Difficulty of Studying the State'.

[19] Ibid., p. 30.

But equally important in creating the state as object is the self-referring nature of knowledge that such a performative view of language presupposes. When discussing terms such as target and leader or social institutions, these are what they are, not because of their physical properties as such, but because of the context of action and belief that rings about them: they are status terms determining our orientation towards objects. As Barnes notes, 'Beliefs about the status of individuals or entities in society are accordingly not fully independent of that to which they refer. To come to believe something about the status of an individual or an entity is to do two things at once: it is to accept a claim about his or its status and at the same time to contribute to the constitution of that status'.[20] Social life and social interactions are essentially constituted by a form of 'bootstrapped induction', which is recursive, and in which much activity is self-referring, and much inference in terms of the local validity of knowledge, is a self-validating contributing to the formation of stable institutional forms. Social life is akin to a monumental self-fulfilling prophecy. [21]

Thus, the state is not a thing or something you lay your hands on, but a reality that exists in its effects and the collective beliefs which underpin these effects. The state exists differently to how people believe it exists: it is not an entity but an administrative or bureaucratic field, part of the field of power, a space structured according to oppositions linked to specific forms of capital tied to different social interests. In addition to claiming the state has a monopoly over legitimate physical and symbolic violence, and regarding the state as a 'bureaucratic' or 'administrative field,' Bourdieu also argues that it is the 'central bank of symbolic capital', the place where a monopoly of legitimate symbolic violence has been established:

What I want t try to show is how a great fetish like the state was constituted, or to use a metaphor that I shall go on to explain, "this central bank of symbolic capital", this kind of site where all the fiduciary currency circulating in the social world is produced and guaranteed, as well as all the realities we can designate as fetishes, whether an educational qualification, a legitimate culture, the nation, the notion of state border, or spelling.[22]

---

[20] Barnes, *Power*, p. 88.

[21] Barnes, Barry, *Sociology*, Vol 17. no. 4 1983 pp. 524–525.

[22] Bourdieu, *On the State*. pp. 122–3.

ACTS OF STATE

In order to break through the illusion of its theological reality, Bourdieu suggests that we can de-reify the state by examining the mechanisms that produce *state effects*. This entails substituting for the idea of the state, 'acts of state'. Part of the power of the state exists in the power of its performative discourse, its authority, in terms of official declarations, its power of naming and judging. The concentration and monopoly of symbolic capital allows the state, as a central bank of capital, an almost magical power not only to provide titles, make official declarations but also to endorse and back all acts of nomination, credentials and guarantees – making both positive and negative judgments, and solidifying and consecrating extant social divisions in the social world. It also provides symbolic authority to state agents who act and speak on its behalf, who are mandated to speak for it – *prosopopoeia*. This becomes evident if we compare a private insult with a judgment made by an authorised person, such as a teacher, whose discourse, because reflecting the position of a state sanctioned functionary, carries greater force and has important social effects. Bourdieu gives the following example: when a relative says 'you are an idiot' this is a reversible, singular judgment by a single individual to which one can respond with a reciprocal insult; whereas if a teacher, even euphemistically, says that 'your son is an idiot' this is a judgment backed by the state 'with the whole force of the social order behind it'.[23]

If we regress and try to understand the foundation of this authority of state delegates, those mandated to speak on behalf of the state, we ultimately reach the state, as what Marx calls an 'illusory community' and as a holder of symbolic power:

> [A]cts of state . . . have in common the fact of being actions performed by state agents endowed with symbolic authority, and followed by effects. This symbolic authority refers, step by step, to a kind of illusory community, a kind of ultimate consensus. If these acts obtain consent, if people accept them – even if they rebel, their rebellion presupposes a consent – it is because, at bottom, they consciously or unconsciously participate in a kind of 'illusory community' – that is an expression of Marx's about the state – which is the community of belonging to a community that we shall call a nation or a state, in the sense of a set of people recognizing the same universal principles.[24]

---

[23] Ibid., p. 61.

[24] Ibid., p. 12.

The state is effectively equivalent to Aristotle's God, 'the unmoved mover'.

> Here then we have examples of acts of state: these are authorized acts, endowed with an authority that, by a series of delegations, goes back step by step to an ultimate site, like Aristotle's god: the state. Who guarantees the teacher? What guarantees the teacher's judgment? A similar regression can also be traced in quite other domains. If you take the judgments of justice, it is still more evident; similarly, if you take the investigating report of a policeman, the regulations drawn up by a commission or laid down by a minister. In all these cases, we are faced with acts of categorization; the etymology of the word 'category' – from *categorein* – means publicly accusing, even insulting; state *categorien* publicly accuses with public authority: 'I publicly accuse you of being guilty'; 'I publicly certify that you are a university agrege'; 'I categorize you' (the accusation may be positive or negative); 'I sanction you', with an authority that authorizes both the judgment and, evidently, the categories according to which the judgment is made.[25]

A further critical and defining feature of the state is the notion that it embodies a public power – *res-publica*. State action is by definition public as rather than private. Public problems are problems to be dealt with officially, in public space, the open so to speak.

THE POWER OF NAMING, DELEGATION, THE PUBLIC AND ACTING FOR THE UNIVERSAL INTEREST

In examining acts of state, Bourdieu discusses the 'magical alchemy' through which individuals are transformed by the power of state delegation, and naming, into mandatories – state officials empowered to speak using official speech on behalf of the public and universal. This is supplemented by the role of rhetoric, theatricality and a special lexica. Following Kantorowicz, he refers to this as 'the mystery of ministry'.[26] The authority given to the agent

---

[25] Ibid., p. 11.

[26] Ibid., p. 34. See also Bourdieu, Pierre. 'The Mystery of Ministry: From Particular Wills to the General Will' in Wacquant (ed.) *Pierre Bourdieu and Democratic Politics: The Mystery of Ministry*. Cambridge: Polity, 2005, pp. 55–63.

representing the state constitutes 'the alchemy of representation' whereby 'the representative makes the group which makes him'.[27] This is seen clearly for instance in the role of Commissions such as the Barre Housing Commission in France, which is discussed in some detail in *The Social Structures of the Economy*.[28] Such Commissions, as entities which are generated and mandated by the state, contain officials who purportedly engage with and speak on behalf of the public and in the name of the universal. Thus, underpinning the authority of the modern state and its ability to delegate to official agents is a fundamental belief that the state represents public service and disinterestedness, a neutral arbiter standing for the universal interest and collective good. This persistent trope of disinterestedness both depends upon and reproduces the idea that the state can stand apart from the range of partial and partisan perspectives linked to specific social interests. A viewpoint encompassing all viewpoints, the state's eye has ultimately no perspective at all and as such is akin to Leibniz's notion of God, 'the geometrical of all perspectives'.[29] The role of the official is thereby identified essentially by disinterestedness, of acting on behalf of the public, the universal interest of society and not on the basis of self-interest.

Of the two sense of the state often discussed in dictionaries – the restricted and secondary sense of an administration, form of government, set of public powers and bureaucratic institutions, on the one hand, and the state, primarily as a nationally unified territory, with citizens who speak the same language etc., on the other, it is the former that creates the latter. This, according to Bourdieu, runs against our ordinary or naive understanding, which as a consequence of fetishism, perceives the causal explanation in the opposite direction. The bureaucratic state creates civil society and not vice versa. This has implications for debates concerning the state and nation which constitute false debates. For Bourdieu, the state/civil society dichotomy, which is pervasive in Marxist and other analyses of the state, should he asserts be abandoned and replaced with a focus on values and access to state resources:

> The distinction between state 1 as government, public service, public powers, and state 2 as the entire people that this state has as its base, should be

---

[27] Bourdieu, *Language and Symbolic*, p. 106.

[28] Bourdieu, Pierre. *The Social Structures of the Economy*. Cambridge: Polity, 2005.

[29] *On the State*, p. 28.

challenged and replaced by a distinction in terms of degree. Maurice Halbwachs spoke of the "focus of cultural values" from which people are more or less removed; it would be possible to speak of a 'focus on state values' and establish a fairly simple index of a linear hierarchy of distance from the focus of state values by taking for example, the capacity to make interventions, to absolve contraventions etc. A cumulative index could be arrived at, more or less rigorous, of the differential proximity of different social agents to the centre of state-type resources: one could also introduce an index of proximity in mental structures. I would tend to substitute, for the simple opposition of state and civil society, the idea of a continuum which is a continuous distribution of access to the collective, to the public resources, material or symbolic, with which the name "state" is associated. This distribution, like all distributions in all social worlds, is the basis of constant struggles.[30]

Such a conceptualization both draws on Durkheim's theory of the state and modifies it. Like Durkheim, the major criterion distinguishing states is not their form of constitution whether monarchy or democracy, but the degree to which state thought has penetrated the collective conscience and transformed it so that it was clear and reflective rather than opaque and habitual. Likewise Bourdieu is less concerned with the specific modality of constitutions or politics in the strict sense, than in state thinking as a form that shapes people's thought and the degree to which it does so. With Durkheim, he also seems to exclude the government and politicians from his definition of the state, discussing the political field as a semi-autonomous space.[31] However, as some commentators have pointed out, this is ambiguous and their precise relation remains unclear.[32] Nevertheless, although not discussing the exact articulation between them, what they share and what is at stake in the political field is a monopoly of the legitimate principle of (di)vision of the social world including a struggle over the 'power over the "public

---

[30] *On the State*, p. 36.

[31] 'Political Representation: Elements for a Theory of the Political Field' in *Language and Symbolic Power*. Cambridge: Polity, pp. 171–202.

[32] Schinkel, Willem. 'The Sociologists and the State: An Assessment of Pierre Bourdieu's Sociology' *British Journal of Sociology*, 66 (2). 2015, pp. 222–223; Jessop, Bob. 'The Central Bank of Symbolic Capital' *Radical Philosophy*, 193. Sept/Oct. 2015, pp. 33–41.

powers" (state administrations)'.[33] In the political field, politicians as professional representatives of social classes, who delegate them, have their affiliation mediated by their relation to other politicians with whom they are in competition. Symbolic capital is central in such relationships. In parliamentary democracies, politicians belong to political parties engaged in a 'sublimated form of civil war' who aim to mobilise as many agents as possible with the same vision of the social world, and its future, in order to gain power. Here, their morally/ politically informed visions of the social world remain secondary to the acquisition of power. The struggle of political parties to win as many votes as possible is simultaneously a conflict over retaining or altering the distribution of power over public powers – the police, army, law and public finances.

[33] Bourdieu, *Political Representation*, p. 181.

CHAPTER 5

The State and the Field of Power

Abstract This chapter discusses how Bourdieu envisages the state as part of the field of power. It discusses his work on the state nobility and examines the state as part of a meta field possessing meta capital.

Keywords Field of power · State nobility · Social reproduction · Consecration · Nomination

Social structures, as Bourdieu points out, exist twice: in both the 'objectivity of the first order', constituted as objective social positions and in 'the objectivity of the second order', in the form of systems of classification, and subjective bundles of dispositions and cognitive schemata which inform people's thoughts, feelings and conduct. Social divisions are, therefore, inscribed in both the material order viz-viz differential and hierarchical distributions, and in the symbolic order, through discourses and cognitive classifications. States therefore have both material and ideological aspects. The 'objective' institutional features of the state which includes the civil service, the schools, the welfare state and various authorities that through their *practices* administer the life chances and shape the destinies of those within its territorial area, need to be conjoined with the state's symbolic and ideological role of shaping and constituting people's social identities, and their thinking. In structuring people's ways of thinking, acting and feeling to use Durkheim's Kantian phrase, the state combines a symbolic and

© The Author(s) 2017   83
S. Loyal, *Bourdieu's Theory of the State*,
DOI 10.1057/978-1-137-58350-5_5

expressive dimension with a materialist and instrumentalist one. Yet, it is the cognitive, ideational and symbolic component that retains causal and explanatory primacy in his writing.

Discourses and schemes of classification, through the fostering and reproduction of restricted narratives of ethnic and national identity and nationalism, but equally through the codification, collection, control and storage of information as a means for monitoring and regulating a circumscribed population, become instilled in individuals and embedded in their practical relation to the world. States as we noted in the last chapter, have not only monopolised physical force and taxation but more importantly the legitimate use of symbolic force, including the power to name, to categorise and to define objects and events.

This ability to regulate social life of course depends in part upon the state's capacity to sustain and impose categories of thought through which institutions and individuals make sense of the world. This is a form of 'worldmaking'.[1] Political struggle is a cognitive struggle for the power to impose the legitimate vision of the social world – that is, the power to (re)make reality by establishing, preserving or altering the categories through which agents comprehend and construct that world.[2] By providing categories and accepted ways of thinking that people inherit and necessarily have to make reference to, these individuals recursively and for the most part unintentionally reproduce the social classificatory system.

As was stated earlier Bourdieu depicts the state not as a clearly bounded, unitary entity – this is, a screen discourse it produces – but rather as a field of competing forces in which various agents compete over the distribution of public goods and power. In another text he also points to its ability to impose shared coercive norms within a territory:

> In fact, what we encounter, concretely, is an ensemble of administrative or bureaucratic fields (they often take the empirical form of commissions, bureaus and boards) within which agents and categories of agents, governmental and nongovernmental, struggle over this particular form of authority consisting of the power to rule via legislation, regulations, administrative

---

[1] N. Goodman, *Ways of Worldmaking,* Indianapolis: Hacket, 1978.

[2] In terms of the latter, the potential to impose a 'vision of divisions', is the, 'power of making social divisions and hence the political power *par excellence'* Bourdieu *Distinction*, p. 468.

measures (subsidies, authorizations, restrictions etc.) in short, everything that we normally put under the rubric of state policy...The state then, if you insist on keeping this designation, would be the ensemble of fields that are the site of struggles in which what is at stake is-to build on Max Weber's famed formulation – the monopoly of legitimate symbolic violence, i.e. the power to constitute and impose as universal and universally applicable within a given 'nation', that is, within the boundaries of a given territory, a common set of coercive norms.[3]

THE STATE AND THE FIELD OF POWER

We have seen that Bourdieu operates at a number of different levels of abstraction and attempts to give the state a number of definitions including possessing a monopoly on the legitimate use of physical and symbolic violence, as the central bank of symbolic credit and as an internally divided bureaucratic or administrative field of forces. In *On the State* and in the *State Nobility*, Bourdieu also introduces and elaborates upon the state as an integral part of the 'field of power'. The latter concept first appears in a 1971 essay '*Champ du pouvoir, champ intellectuel habitus de classe*' where it is defined as 'the objective structure of relations established between systems of agents and authorities that tend to maintain the established structure of relations between classes'.[4] In its subsequent usage Bourdieu argues that this concept not only demarcates his relational approach from 'substantialist' Marxists theories of the ruling class and functionalist and liberal theories of the elite, both of which tend to focus on individual agents who occupy positions of power, but also to account for forms of power that can be exercised across fields, especially forms of economic and cultural capital. Like all social fields, the field of power is simultaneously a field of forces and a field of struggles that retains a relative autonomy in relation to other fields, and where the different forms of capital are active as both trumps and stakes. Unlike other fields, however, the logic of the field of power is not to accumulate or monopolise a certain kind of capital in

[3] Bourdieu and Wacquant, *An Invitation to Reflexive Sociology*, Chicago: University of Chicago Press, pp. 111–112.

[4] Cited in Champagne et al. 'position of the lectures in Pierre Bourdieu's work' in *On the State*, 2014, p. 409.

its own right. What is involved instead is rather a distinctive kind of balancing or arbitrage: namely, '[the] determination of the relative value and magnitude of the different forms of power that can be wielded in the different fields, or, if you will, power over the different forms of power or the capital granting power over capital'.[5] The field of forces is therefore a space where those with high levels of economic, or cultural capital, or both struggle over the imposition of the dominant form of capital in social space – the 'dominant principle of domination', and simultaneously, the mechanisms aimed at maintaining or altering these forms of capital – the 'dominant principle of legitimation' – either through familial reproduction as in most earlier undifferentiated societies, or school-mediated reproduction which predominates in modern differentiated societies. There is thus a struggle *within* the dominant class fractions in social space, rather than *between* social classes – for example, the dominant class and working class, over the 'conversion' or 'exchange rate' between different forms of capital. The field of power is:

> inseparably, a field of power struggles among the holders of different forms of power, a gaming space in which these agents and institutions possessing enough specific capital (economic or cultural capital in particular) to be able to occupy the dominant positions within their respective fields confront each other using strategies aimed at preserving or transforming these relations of power. The forces that can be enlisted in these struggles, and the orientation given to them, be it conservative or subversive, depend on what might be called the 'exchange rate' (or 'conversion rate') that obtains among the different forms of capital, in other words, on the very thing that these strategies aim to preserve or transform (principally through the defense or criticism of representations of the different forms of capital and their legitimacy.[6]

When viewed as a totality the field of power appears to include those social agents endowed with high levels of economic and cultural capital – large business owners, the Episcopate, the university, employers, higher civil servants in the French state bureaucracy, intellectuals and artists.[7]

---

[5] Bourdieu, *The State Nobility*, p. 265.

[6] Boudieu, *The State Nobility*, pp. 264–265.

[7] Wacquant and Bourdieu, *From Ruling Class*, p. 20; See also Wacquant, Loic. 'Symbolic Power in the Rule of the State Nobility' in Loic Wacquant (ed.) *Pierre Bourdieu and Democratic Politics: the Mystery of Ministry*. Cambridge: Polity, 2005, p. 143.

Positions within the field can only be occupied when individuals not only possess the requisite levels of various forms of capital but also the appropriate desire and habitus.

Bourdieu conceives the field of power as expressing a historical state of social relations that took their present form at the end of the 1880s. Characterised by two diametrically opposed poles – a temporal pole and a spiritual pole – these are occupied in modern times, on the one side by those who benefit from high levels of economic capital and low amounts of cultural capital – the business man – and inversely, those individuals possessing significant levels of cultural capital and limited quantities of economic capital – the intellectual, on the other. Each pole has endemic laws of acquisition, accumulation and transmission of capital. Situated at the midpoint in this chiasmatic structure are those individuals holding both forms of capital, professions and upper level state bureaucrats. In this schema then, the field of power stretches on a continuum from the dominant economic field to the dominated dominant artistic field, with the juridical field, bureaucratic, academic and scientific fields, holding an intermediary position. Each of the sub-fields in the field are organised according to a chiasmatic structure homologous to it. That is, each component field and sub-field contains on the one side the economically or temporally dominant pole and culturally dominated positions, and at the other the culturally or spiritually dominant and economically dominated positions.

According to Bourdieu, the opposition between economic and cultural capital is an old, almost quasi-universal binary part of a *division of labour of domination*. This division is captured in George Duby's distinction between *oratores* and *bellatores* in medieval society – between temporal power and cultural power – or religious capital and military capital.[8] Nevertheless, the opposition varies from society to society in terms of the distance between the given poles, the level of conflict between them, and the degree to which the intellectual pole is subordinated to the economic pole. Since Bourdieu believes that no power can be based on

---

[8] 'If we admit that *the structure of the field of power depends at every moment in the forms of capital engaged in struggles over their respective weight within the structure,* it remains that the fundamental opposition of the division of labour of domination is that between temporal and spiritual powers' Wacquant and Bourdieu, *From Ruling Class*, p. 24.

naked force alone, in modern differentiated societies there operates an *organic solidarity in the division of labour of domination* whereby the dominant groupings in the social order must wield several different forms of power to consolidate their social position.

The contemporary struggle between businessmen (industrial knights) and intellectuals has, he believes, been shaped by two fundamental developments, especially within the administrative and economic field, that have taken place in the struggle 'for power over power'. Their compund effect has been to alter the exchange rate between the different forms of capital. The first has been a relative increase in the importance of academic titles in relation to property titles; the second a relative decline in technical titles with respect to titles guaranteeing general bureaucratic training. These changes have been expressed in the shift in reproduction strategies employed by dominant groups and classes which include *inter alia*: fertility strategies, inheritance strategies, education strategies, prophylactic strategies, economic strategies, marriage strategies and sociodicy strategies. Most significantly, school-mediated reproduction strategies entailing educational credentials have become increasingly necessary even for the 'business bourgeoisie', especially as the age and size of the firm increases. This has not precipitated a disappearance of the familial mode of reproduction; rather, its amalgamation with school-mediated reproduction has become imperative. This, in turn, has generated struggles over the stakes involved in the educational system between the temporal and spiritual powers. It is here that the state, as the administrative field located between the two poles, plays a central role not only by setting the conversion rate between capitals but also through the provision of titles specifically viz-a-viz the *grandes écoles*, by consecrating individuals. It is through the state conferral of titles and naming – degrees, certificates, knighthoods, appointment of offices, posts or honours – that rites of institution have their most powerful effects.

ACADEMIC TITLES

Those who take up the highest positions in the state or bureaucratic field – the new state nobility – differ in their mode of reproduction from other status groups (*Stände*), not only in terms of a statistical logic which ensures that certain individuals from this elite cadre fail but also because they are linked to the state through their academic titles. The academic title constitutes a public and official warranty given by a recognised collective authority – the state – which 'objectively' guarantees a competence. These technical qualifications are inalienable and, unlike property and offices, cannot be hereditarily transferred: they confer privileges, warrant specific functions and income, and provide their holders a legal monopoly backed by the authority of the state. The academic title exemplifies a form of *state magic* which consecrates a state of affairs while appearing to record them, in the process transforming the nature of the individual: 'These acts of official recording, in the guise of taking note of a *de facto* situation (a relation between two people, occupying a certain position, being ill or disabled etc.) cause this situation to undergo a genuine ontological promotion, a transmutation, a change of nature or essence'.[9]

There is then an essential link between the state bureaucracy and academic titles. State sanctioned academic titles and expertise facilitate the formation of a 'privileged "caste"'. Drawing on his philosophical anthropology based on the struggle for recognition, Bourdieu avers that rites of institution exercise their power because they give individuals an appearance of meaning, 'giving them a feeling of having a role or, quite simply, some importance, and thus tearing them from the clutches of insignificance...they manage to make consecrated individuals believe that their existence is justified, that their existence serves some purpose'.[10] The elevation of a distinguished class to the level of *Being*, is correlative with the fall of a 'complementary class into Nothingness or the lowest Being'.[11] The titles conferred by the state not only emphatically alter the nature or essence of the person but radically transforms their self-perception as they adapt themselves to what they *should* be. Although they appear trivial, these processes have important consequences: 'Operations of regularisation, such as recognizing a child, or, quite simply recording its birth, or marriage, or still yet, confirming someone in a temporary or acting position are so many bureaucratic maneuvers that, in a way, change nothing, and, in another sense, change everything, specially the collectively attributed meaning and publicly recognized social value of the act or thing in question, with very real consequences: the right to an inheritance, the dependents' allowances, to disability pensions, to sick leave, etc.'[12]

---

[9] Ibid., p. 376.
[10] Bourdieu, *Language*, p. 126.
[11] Ibid.
[12] *The State Nobility*, p. 376.

Despite using the language and rhetoric of universality in their discourse, the state nobility nevertheless pursues strategies to further its own position in social space, and to monopolise higher education positions for its own offspring.

STRUCTURAL HOMOLOGY

Within the field of higher education, the *grandes écoles* play a central role in the reproduction of the field of power viz-a-viz the structural homology that exists between the two social spheres. Students are channelled towards the educational institution suited to their dispositions, since as social agents they 'statistically tend to recognize only those authorities that recognize them'.[13]

Examining the work of consecration carried out by the *grandes écoles* in France, and the preparatory classes that ready and train students for access to positions of power and leadership, allows Bourdieu to reveal *inter alia* the ascetic habitus of the dominant ruling classes in contemporary societies, the variegated and differentiated nature and structure of the power they possess, and the mechanisms of reproduction which legitimate and secure their position. In a process cloaked under the democratic ideology of merit and natural gifts, the blood nobility of birth and nature has become replaced by a school or 'state nobility'. More specifically, the preparatory classes institute an impassable social break, through acts of consecration, creating a distinct status group separated from the commonplace. Effectively operating as Goffmanian 'total institutions', acts of consecration and the performance of rites of institution produces a separate, elevated, sacred group – initially a school and later a state nobility.

Such a mechanism of reproduction reinstitutes a structure of distances and differences between individuals. The logic of the operation of the *grandes écoles* is, for Bourdieu, not so different to the logic operating in the *ancien regime*. Between them, the different *grandes écoles* produce social identities that are simultaneously in competition and complementary a *grand corps* who, in their future role in the field of power, are tied together by an organic solidarity allowing them to maintain a division of labour of domination. They are both divided but simultaneously in

---

[13] Ibid., p. 141.

an antagonistic compact, as 'hostile brothers' conjoined in opposition against the dominated:

> Thus in France, the equivalent of the mechanisms of succession designed to prevent fratricidal struggles between heirs is the division between the *grandes écoles* with, at the one end, the 'intellectual' schools (the *École normale supérieure* and, to a lesser extent, the *École polytechnique*) and, at the other end, the schools which groom for economic power (the *École des hautes etudes commerciales* and other graduate business schools), with, between the two, a school like the *École nationale d'administration*, which opens the way to positions of leadership within state bureaucracies. By distributing young people of different origins among the different schools, each of which presents as both excellent and incomparable, and each according a priority to one particular species of capital, the system produces incomparable forms of excellence and, by the same token, a sort of armed peace between 'hostile brothers'. [14]

Thus an antipathetic system of mutual recognition and competition is effected by an otherwise fractured power holding class in modern society. This is to some extent regulated by the state through its conversion mechanisms and setting of the exchange rate between capitals. The process of elite reproduction not only entails creating a 'business bourgeoisie' who will hold power over positions in large firms, but through the *École nationale d'administration*, the generation of a state bourgeoisie, some of whom will undoubtedly hold positions in large state-owned businesses while others, will take up positions in the higher civil service or become central wielders of power in the administrative or bureaucratic field, that is, the state. The state nobility possesses a specific ascetic habitus acquired by working under the sign or urgency and competition in the *grandes écoles*, this provides them with public proof of self-control, and the right and ability to control others once in power. It also furnishes the *dispositions* necessary for filling social *positions* and underpins their claim to act as disinterested agents acting on behalf of the universal interest. It is the state nobility who constitute the key personnel, as higher civil servants, within the bureaucratic field especially

---

[14] Wacquant and Bourdieu, *From Ruling Class*, p. 22.

taking – up prominent positions in the 'right hand of the state' – which includes the ministries of finance, security etc. Entry and access to the field containing statutorily defined posts is strictly controlled by formal legal rules, educational requirements, certificates, titles etc. or by acts of nomination and invitation. The administrative field contains a variety of social positions defined relationally and differentially to one another – higher level, mid-level and lower level civil servants or upper and lower level state nobility – with varying quantities and compositions of capital, who stand in disparate relations of conflict, competition and cooperation. State departments and personnel are structured in homology with the field of power with dominant economic and dominated dominant cultural capital representing different fractions of the dominants, but who simultaneously hold their own field specific forms of bureaucratic and administrative power – a 'statist' or *meta* capital.

Despite the diverse set of powers and resources – property titles, academic titles, even noble titles – that the new state nobility has in comparison to the earlier nobility, it nevertheless has to bind itself to the idea of competence and devotion to the 'public' or 'universal' in order to sustain its legitimacy. This means acting for the state or nation rather than according to business interests, basing their decisions on 'neutrality' and 'expertise' and following the ethos of 'public service'. Asserting a sociological law, Bourdieu argues, that their actions possess less legitimacy the more they appear to be determined by external physical, economic, political or affective constraints.

THE STATE AS A META-FIELD

This view of the state as one facet or sector within of the field of power – between an economically dominant pole and a culturally dominated – dominant pole, discussed principally in *The State Nobility*, does not sit easily with the views of the state contained in *On the State* which tends to give the state a much greater focus and determining power in shaping, structuring and providing cohesion and consensus in the social world. Nevertheless, the bureaucratic field has the capacity to determine the conversion rate of the various capitals within the field of power, and therefore the ability to condition and structure other social fields. In this sense, the state, as a bureaucratic field, is a 'meta-field', wielding a form of meta-power or power over powers. It is 'meta' since it possesses a 'meta-capital', a capital over capitals, a power which is above all, official and legitimated. As he notes:

> Concentration of the different species of capital (which proceeds hand in hand with the construction of the corresponding fields) leads indeed to the *emergence* of a specific, properly statist capital (*capital étatique*) which enables the state to exercise power over the different fields and over the different particular species of capital, and especially over the rates of conversion between them (and thereby over the relations of force between the respective holders). If follows that the construction of the state proceeds apace with the construction of a *field of power*, defined as the space of play within which the holders of capital (of different species) struggle in particular for power over the state, i.e. over the statist capital granting power over the different species of capital and over their reproduction (particularly through the school system).[15]

The state is both a stake to be fought over in a struggle, and the dominant meta-force that has power over other fields. Such a conception allows us to reflect upon both the origin, structure and the relations between the numerous semi-autonomous fields that constitute the totality of 'social space' in Bourdieu's writings. As Steimetz notes: 'Given the state's dominance over other fields, it follows that the state is the precondition of the differentiation of society into multiple, semi-autonomous fields and the site of struggles over those fields'.[16] The relationships between social fields are therefore not simply ordered in terms of homology, but are hierarchically structured according to the field of power both through homology and by the state setting the conversion rate between various capitals – principally economic and cultural capital as generic forms of power – that can be exercised in various fields.

---

[15] Bourdieu, *Rethinking*, pp. 4–5.

[16] Steinmetz, George. 'On Bourdieu, Sur l'Etat: Field Theory and the State, Colonies, and Empires' *Sociologica*, 3.2014, p. 3.

As Champagne et al note: 'one could put forward the idea that the state is the almost necessary product of a double process: on the one hand, the differentiation of societies into relatively autonomous fields, and on the other, the emergence of a space that concentrates powers over the latter, and in which the struggles are between the fields themselves, between the new agents of history'. p. 380.

It could be argued the view that the field of power structures and delimits the contours and dynamics of other social fields – the economic, political, educational, intellectual, cultural field etc. – through homology, tends to overstate a structural order that should perhaps be open to empirical analysis. Of course, Bourdieu argues that fields need to be studied empirically but in the context of this rather rigid homology and chiasmatic structure. Here, there needs to be a mediating position between such a strong structuralist viewpoint and the kind of Weberian argument that focuses on contingency found, for example, in the work of Michael Mann where the state and social order is envisaged as essentially 'a cock up'.[17]

---

[17] Mann, *Social Sources Volume II*, p. 52.

CHAPTER 6

State Formation

Abstract This chapter outlines Bourdieu's theory of state formation. This entails examining the development of the state from the twelfth century to modern-day contemporary society. Bourdieu talks about four stages in state formation involving the concentration of various capitals and the development of a state bureaucracy with an interest in pursuing the public interest, or universal.

Keywords State formation · Bureaucracy · Patrimonialism · Struggle · Juridical field

An analysis of what the state consists of and what it does presupposes an historical analysis of its emergence. For example, How did the state acquire the monopoly of legitimate physical and symbolic violence? In addition to examining 'state acts', for Bourdieu, a genetic structuralist methodology can break through state *doxa* allowing us to perceive the 'arbitrariness of beginnings'. Such a methodology does not mean establishing a straightforward historical or comparative analysis but, rather, constructing a theoretical *model* of the state that allows statements about the state to be open to systematic verification. Here, France, and to a lesser extent England, function as privileged examples of possible cases of more universal state processes, countries that also served in reality as models for the development of subsequent modern states. Bourdieu attempts to show

© The Author(s) 2017
S. Loyal, *Bourdieu's Theory of the State,*
DOI 10.1057/978-1-137-58350-5_6

how an autonomous bureaucratic field with its own specific logic and capital or *raison d'etat* emerged. Drawing primarily on secondary analyses of state-formation starting from the twelfth century, modern states, he argues, did not emerge until after the seventeenth century, differ fundamentally from earlier states, including city-states and empires, and dynastic or patrimonial states.

In his analysis of state formation, Bourdieu foregrounds the process of the initial accumulation of *symbolic* capital in contrast to what he considers are physicalist Marxist approaches that well solely on the agglomeration of economic or material resources. Bourdieu signals that his approach, especially in dealing with the conditions in which this initial accumulation took place, shares strong similarities with Hegel's discussion of the master–slave relationship that places a social contract at its origin. For Bourdieu, initial accumulation is an extraordinary phenomenon in which 'a certain number of people abandon the power of judging in the last instance, and receive from other people an abdication in relation to certain very important things – the right to make peace and war, to say who is guilty or not guilty, who is a real advocate or real builder. We find ourselves today in a state of the state where these things are taken for granted'.[1] This form of alienation as abdication and delegation is discussed in some detail in his essay on Delegation and Political Fetishism.[2]

Bourdieu outlines a model based on four stages of state formation that are both logical and chronological.[3] The first stage concerns the process of concentration of each type of capital – military, informational (cultural) and economic – which form part of the process of the monopolisation of symbolic capital. Within his materialist theory of the symbolic, although all capitals are interdependent and together form a whole, symbolic capital both constitutes a pre-condition for the other capitals and accumulates alongside them. This aggregation, which takes place with the birth of the dynastic state, is not simply of accretion but, generates emergent properties, which when combined transmute to eventually create a '*meta*' or state capital: making the state *meta*, a

---

[1] Ibid., 70.

[2] Bourdieu, Pierre. 'Delegation and Political Fetishism' In *Language and Symbolic Power,* pp. 203–219.

[3] *On the State,* pp. 213–214.

power above powers as discussed earlier. This allows a distinction to emerge between those who hold a specific capital, and those who retain a power over all capitals, via the state. The state becomes a central bank of symbolic capital, and as a field of power endowed with a state capital, maintains control over all the other social fields as well as the rate of conversion between them.

THE CONCENTRATION OF CAPITALS

The Monopolisation of Physical Capital

The establishment of the state as a unified national-social space, a space of spaces or field of fields, holding a meta or state capital occurs co-extensively with the emergence and establishment of differentiated and relatively autonomous social fields, such as the economic and cultural field or market, initially during the twelfth century. This process also entails the concentration and monopolisation of physical capital. Two inter-related processes here are central: the external need to wage war abroad to acquire more land and territory, and the internal requirement to oppose competing lords, and those from the lower classes, which leads to the development of centralised military and police forces respectively: 'these two factors favour the creation of powerful armies within which specifically military forces are gradually distinguished from specifically police forces intended to maintain internal order'.[4] Here Bourdieu concurs with, and draws upon, Elias's argument that the concentration of public physical force was accompanied by a reduction and control of day-to-day violence. Again such processes presuppose the prior accumulation of symbolic capital – for example, the concentration of physical violence into a specialised body with symbolic uniforms – the police – processes of mobilisation can only occur if the state has some prior legitimacy.

The Monopolisation of Taxation

The concentration of the means of violence is accompanied by a mono-polisation of taxation and eventually the construction and centralisation of economic capital. In the last decade of the twelfth century an impersonal

---

[4] *On the State*, p. 200.

tax paid by all subjects and required for territorial defence increasingly became used as a justification for imposing more general public tax levies. A system of tax collection was instituted whereby mandates in the form of uniformed and qualified liveries as representatives of the state were authorised to collect taxes. The authoritative, legitimated, and official nature of taxation also became bound up with the rise of an elementary form of patriotism or quasi-nationalism.

This process underwrote a division between the injustice and corruption of tax collectors, and the ideal of justice embodied in the king, which was to become one of 'the principles of the genesis of the idea of the state as an instance transcending the agents who embody it'.[5] Such a bifurcation subsequently generated the idea of a transcendent state, rising above sectional interests and perceived as a continuous, abstract entity.

To function effectively taxation also required an efficient financial system containing accounting, verification and an assessment of the number of properties within a delimited territory to be undertaken by an emerging bureaucracy. Holding the power of informational capital such a nascent bureucracy generated the birth of a regime in which *stat*istics became integrally linked to the *stat*e: 'It is not by chance that the state's instrument par excellence is statistics. Statistics make it possible to totalize information from individuals and obtain from this, totalization, information that none of the individuals who provided the basic information have'.[6] Here, as with the work of Elias, the relationship between taxation and warfare was one of circular causality wherein taxes were used for war and the funding of armies which in turn presupposed additional taxation and informational capital. The prior accumulation of symbolic capital here served as a basis upon which the legitimate appropriation of taxation could be effected. In the words of Elias the state became a 'legitimate racket', offering protection in return for money.

The Concentration of Cultural Capital

This process of unification, centralisation and monopolisation in terms of military and economic forces was also one of standardisation and homogenisation, through the creation of an autonomous and centralised cultural

---

[5] *On the State*, p. 204.

[6] Ibid., p. 214.

market. The unification of culture, in parallel with the development of an economic market, entailed the creation of a legitimate *national* culture containing standardised and generalised knowledge such as: educational qualifications, weights and measurements, common writing and spelling practices. Here, cultural capital constitutes one dimension of a more generic form of informational capital. The state begins to measure, assess, investigate and concentrate information, regulating its distribution, instigating the birth of maps, drawing up genealogies, and unifying theories. These acts, which presuppose writing, take place, metaphorically speaking, from an elevated position encompassing the viewpoint of totalisation: 'The state is the unitary, overhead viewpoint on a space that is unified theoretically and homogenized by the act of construction. Basically this is Cartesian space'.[7] Such a process ultimately involves the homogenisation and normalisation of individuals: by concentrating culture the state appropriates and unifies a national cultural habitus.

It is of fundamental significance for Bourdieu that the concentration and universalisation of cultural capital has to be understood as a process inseparable from social domination and dispossession: as the state monopolises the linguistic market it simultaneously downgrades and disqualifies local accents, dialects, in a word all 'improper' languages. Equally, local customs, rights and regional diversity gives way to nationalist forms of cultural concentration and unity. The centralisation of cultural capital is a *national* concentration of cultural capital and symbolic capital.

The Concentration of Juridical Capital

The concentration of juridical capital also takes place in parallel with the concentration of physical/military, economic and cultural and capital. Juridical capital represents an 'objectified and codified form of symbolic capital'.[8] Given that symbolic capital is itself the outcome of other capitals when misrecognised, this is somewhat confusing assertion by Bourdieu. Nevertheless, in this process diverse, mutually exclusive bodies of law including those with ecclesiastical, lay, and seigniorial jurisdictions, and justices of the commons and towns, became increasingly unified from the

---

[7] Ibid.
[8] Bourdieu, *Rethinking*, p. 9.

twelfth century onwards. Judges and jurors of the feudal courts are gradually replaced by provosts, bailiffs, and impersonal professional lawyers, and their decisions increasingly referred to the king. The result is the creation of a separate legal field with its own laws that reflect the advancement of formally universal institutions respecting laws and protecting universal rights. Law thereby becomes a central dimension of symbolic capital.

Monopolisation and Universalisation

The opposition between monopolisation and universalisation constitutes a central feature of the process of state formation. The two processes, though putatively understood as contrary and mutually exclusive, in fact, take place simultaneously:

> We may say that the development of the modern state can be described as a progress towards a higher degree of universalization (de-localization, de-particularizaton etc.) and in the same movement, as a progress towards monopolization, the concentration of power, thus towards the establishment of the conditions of a central domination.[9] In other words the two processes are both linked and contrary.[10]

An initial phase of 'universalizing integration' is followed by a second phase of 'alienating integration', as a condition for domination and dispossession.[11] Integration, therefore, is not opposed to exclusion and subjugation, but actually a condition of it. As capital concentrates it universalises by moving from the local to the national, the particular to the universal, so that it becomes monopolised by a group, allowing a centralised form of domination. This, Bourdieu believes, moves his analysis beyond both Weber and Elias who fail to ask 'who has a monopoly of this monopoly?'[12] The process of statisation as universalisation, therefore, allows a

---

[9] The first face [of the state], therefore, is that of universalising integration; the second phase is that of alienating integration as a condition of domination, subjugation, dispossession. And the two faces are inseparable' *On the State*, p. 227.

[10] *On The State*, p. 222.

[11] Ibid., p. 227.

[12] Ibid., p. 237.

certain group of individuals – the state nobility – to have privileged access to a monopoly of symbolic capital and power.

The Dynastic Patrimonial State – The Second Phase of State Formation

The second phase of state-formation takes place conjointly with the concentration and monopolisation of symbolic capital. This entails an analysis of the dynastic-patrimonial state in which the government, and all major possessions within a territory, are perceived as the personal property of the king. The state here is identified with the 'king's house', which includes the broader royal family household. This conflation of public and private is captured in the apocryphal remark attributed to Louis XIV, that *'L'Etat, c'est moi.'* Although the state is seen as an extension of the king and as his personal possession, the role of the king transcends the individual, who as Kantorowicz (1957) notes,[13] temporally inhabits the institution and is required to perpetuate both the material and symbolic honour of the house, or at least the name of the royal lineage he represents. Reproduction strategies centred on succession and family wars around patrimony, royal blood, and lineage constitute the central dynamic in dynastic states. The king's position of power is reinforced by the fact that he places himself strategically at the 'centre' as feudal chieftan, and becomes the only means through which all other nobles can communicate to one another – what Elias dubbed the 'royal mechanism'.[14]

The combination of sovereignty, acquired through Roman law, and suzerainty provides the king with an initial accumulation of symbolic capital. Here – again drawing on the performative power of discourse and self-referring character of knowledge – Bourdieu argues that by claiming himself king he becomes recognised as king:

> In effect, in accordance with the logic of the 'speculative bubble' dear to the economists, he is found to believe he is a king because the others believe (at least to some extent) that he is king, each having to reckon with the fact that the

---

[13] Kantorowicz, Ernst. *The King's Two Bodies: A Study in Medieval Political Theology.* Princeton: Princeton University Press, 1957.

[14] Elias, Norbert. *The Civilizing Process: Sociogenetic and Psychogenetic Investigations.* 1st ed. Cambridge, MA: Blackwell Publishers, 2000.

others reckon with the fact that he is king. A minimal differential thus suffices to create a maximal gap because it differentiates him from all the others.[15]

As material and symbolic resources (in the form of various species of capital) become concentrated in the king, he selectively distributes favours in the form of money, titles, and indulgences to maintain relations of dependence and to perpetuate his power. Effectively he institutes 'the private appropriation of public resources by a few'.[16] In a situation where personal politics and kin relationships of fealty are dominant, structural corruption becomes rife especially among the lower level delegated authorities.

The nascent bureaucracy remains a personal property of the king and subordinated to the logic of the king's house. It is there to 'serve the king'. However, judicial discourses on the institution of the 'crown' as a principle of sovereignty, over and above and independent of the person of king, result in the social position of the crown becoming an autonomous, revered entity. Within a 'division of labour of domination', and especially the growing inter-dynastic political struggles including rivalries between the king and his brothers and his second sons for power, the king becomes increasingly dependent on bureaucrats. The latter, as individuals possessing a specific competence, based on the legal language of Roman law, help to guarantee his reproduction as heir. This leads to a tri-partite struggle for power:

> One encounters thus, almost universally, a tripartite division of power, with alongside *the king*, the *king's brothers* (in the broad sense), dynastic rivals whose authority rests on the dynastic principle of the house, and the *king's ministers*, typically *homines novi*, 'new men' recruited for their competency. One can say, at the cost of some simplification, that the king needs the ministers to limit and control the power of his brothers and that, conversely, he can use his brothers to limit and control the power of ministers.[17]

In addition to employing officials dependent on him, the king attempts to reproduce his dominant position and that of his household, and to resolve some of the inter-dynastic conflicts by providing *apanages* as land (often acquired through war or marriages) to give to his sons.

---

[15] Bourdieu, *From the King's House*, p. 34.

[16] Ibid., p. 41.

[17] Ibid., p. 37.

Bureaucratic functionaries or oblates are for the most part chosen by the king on the basis that they are unable to reproduce themselves or have few ties of interest in opposition to the king. Frequently coming from marginalised groups, as Weber noted (1978) – clerics vowed to celibacy, eunuchs, and pariahs of low birth, bureaucrats represent the antithesis of the king's brothers in that they are wholly dependent on the king giving him everything, including their loyalty, while aiming to serve the state. Universities, which emerged in the twelfth century and proliferated from the fourteenth century under the patronage of princes, play a crucial role in training these future oblates.

From the King's House to the Reason of the State – The Third Phase of State Formation

The contradictions between the king, his brothers, and the king's ministers – bureaucrats – ushers in the emergence of a new 'statist' third phase that Bourdieu characterises as a move 'from the king's house to *raison d'État*'.[18] Here the *personal* power of the king becomes increasingly diffused and differentiated, eventually leading to the emergence of the *impersonal* power of the modern state. This is a transitional phase characterised by the conflict between two opposing groups and their correlative principles. On the one hand, there exists bearers of the old social model of reproduction deriving from the dynastic state where reproduction continues to be centred on lineage, blood, hereditary and biology, and where the king rules in a personal manner as an extension of the household. On the other hand, there emerges a new model of reproduction, partly as the result of the development of an autonomous legal field, based on acquired competence and merit, in which individuals – specifically lawyers and bureaucrats – have accrued powers independent of the king, and who rule on a detached basis wielding impersonal powers.

The role of the judiciary mentioned in the earlier section on the accumulation of symbolic capital is a central vector in this transitional process. As the field of power differentiates, rising groups of bureaucrats and lawyers argue for universal principles of rule based on law and reason appealing to generic legal principles. This pursuit of the universal within the legal field corresponds with and furthers their own particular interests,

---

[18] Bourdieu, *From the Kings*.

and incrementally undermines previously held notions of legitimacy anchored in hereditary nobility through blood. A new state nobility – the *noblesse de robe* – based on competence, gradually displaces the old blood nobility – the *noblesse d'épée*. The state nobility, initially as the *noblesse de robe*, is depicted by Bourdieu as the 'self-made' product of correlative and complementary inventions tied to its historical development. It was a body that constituted itself and simultaneously the state:

> *The noblesse de robe*, of which contemporary technocrats are the structural heirs (and sometimes the descendants), is a body that created itself by creating the state, a body that, in order to build itself, had to build the state, that is, among other things, an entire political philosophy of 'public service' and service to the state, or to the 'public' – and not simply to the king, as with his former nobility – and of this service as a 'disinterested' activity, directed towards universal ends.[19]

These acts of construction were practical and symbolically constitutive operations that aimed to establish positions of bureaucratic power that were relatively independent from temporal power – the *noblesse d'épée* (noblemen of the sword or knights), and spiritual forms of power – the clergy. They entailed creating a group that acquired its competence through new educational institutions. This was not only expressed in the increase in university populations in the mid-sixteenth and seventeenth centuries with the expansion of church and state bureaucracies, but also later in the eighteenth century, when selected and selective colleges prepared students for military and bureaucratic offices. As dominated dominants holding an ambiguous position in social space, the *noblesse de robe* could only increase its power by associating its causes with universal causes – emancipatory science, or the liberating nature of the school – that is, by holding an interest in disinterestedness. Alongside marriage strategies, educational strategies providing a specific competence became increasingly important as a new modality of reproduction strategy. Together with the ideal of providing 'public service', this competence gave the *noblesse de robe* a privileged relation to the state. These were men of law rather than war, wielding a pen rather than a sword. Such a process of usurpation was steady and piecemeal. Drawing on the work of Francoise Autrand, Bourdieu argues that Parliament was not

---

[19] *The State Nobility*, p. 379.

built by eliminating the old nobility but rather by incorporating some of its principles, including the devotion to public service, which became transposed from serving the king to serving the state. Unlike the hereditary obligations to public service of the old nobility, devotion to the state was a vocation, or a consciously chosen occupation which emerged from dispositions, skills and competence gained from education.

Understanding such a transition in collective perceptions and organisation requires not only drawing on historical accounts but also on historians of ideas, religion and the church, as well as the politico-religious theories produced by many generations of the state nobility: from royal jurists in the Middle ages, to Girondin lawyers, to the Gaullist reformers of the Fifth Republic. These ideologies entailed the creation of a new *sociodicy* in the form of civic humanism: using knowledge and competence as a basis for conduct and taking civic virtue and duties seriously, as part of a political philosophy to serve the nation. Such a view emerges in the writings of Louis the Caron, Louis le Roy and Chancellor d'Aguesseau and can be opposed not only to the individualism and separation of the public and private promulgated by Montaigne and Charron, but also to the viewpoint of royal power and church.

Hence, although the two models of reproduction based on blood and merit initially operate alongside each other, through a long and imperceptible process of defeudalisation, the new state nobility, within an increasingly autonomous bureaucratic field, come to supplant and denegate personal rule. It supersedes this with a form of formal rule independent of politics, and autonomous from economics, based on the idea of disinterestedness, as a specific reason of state. The outcome is the development of an autonomous bureaucratic or administrative field where the distinction between function and functionary, public and private interests, and disinterestedness, becomes a central aspect of the civil servant's habitus and which manifests the operation of a bureaucratic logic. With Elias, the lengthening of chains of interdependency are crucial for this transition to a *raison d'état*:

> One could say, for the sake of a pleasing formula, that the (impersonal state) is the small change of absolutism, as if the king had been dissolved into the impersonal network of a long chain of mandated plenipotentiaries who are answerable to a superior from whom thy receive their authority and their power, but also, to some extent, for him and for the orders they receive from him.[20]

---

[20] *From the King's House*, p. 48.

The lengthening of chains of interdependency and legitimation does not, however, eliminate the potentiality for corruption but rather increases it as a 'centralized patrimonialism' coexists together with a local form of patrimonialism. Nevertheless, it also increases the possibility of enlarging the public and universal interests of citizens generally: as power grows progressively complex and more diverse, and relatively autonomous fields emerge with peculiar forms of capital and a specific logic, formal law becomes steadily institutionalised. The modern state, as we now conceive it, only really comes to being in the seventeenth century in France and England. Governed by a bureaucratic field and embedded within a context of a society retaining a public realm, it is characterised by a 'state-nobility' whose power rests on educational capital and merit, competing over the control of this centralised state or public capital, and the profits that flow from it, as well as their redistribution in terms of employment:

> But the paradox is that the difficult genesis of a public realm comes hand in hand with the appearance and accumulation of a public capital, and with the emergence of the bureaucratic field as a field of struggles for control over this capital and of the corresponding power, in particular power over the redistribution of public resources and their associated profits... The bureaucratic field... becomes the site of a struggle for power over statist capital and over the material profits (salaries, benefits) and symbolic profits (honors, titles etc.) it provides, a struggle reserved in fact for a minority of claimants designated by the quasi-hereditary possession of educational capital.[21]

FROM BUREAUCRATIC STATE TO A WELFARE STATE – THE FOURTH STAGE OF STATE FORMATION

In the fourth stage of state formation, Bourdieu briefly alludes to a shift from a 'bureaucratic state' to a 'welfare state'. This signals a shift in the locus of conflict from struggles over state formation to struggles over acquisition and control of symbolic and other forms of capitals associated with the state. It is a phase foregrounding the relationship between the state, social space and different social classes.

---

[21] Ibid., p. 51.

The process of autonomisation and separation of the power from the person of the king to impersonal bureaucratic forces is not a linear or progressive one as, for example, with Weber's notion of increasing rationalisation. Rather, it evinces an intermittent and gradual development with the constant possibility of regressions to a patrimonial form of state characterised by corruption and misappropriations of authority always being present. According to Bourdieu, this was evident even under more recent left-wing governments in France.

In his discussion of the *State Nobility*, Bourdieu not only demonstrates the continuing conflicts between those who favour school-mediated reproduction and hereditary reproduction, but also asserts that a number of contemporary social struggles and conflicts are not reducible to class conflicts between the dominant and dispossessed. These should instead be interpreted in terms of struggles between a minor state nobility, with moderate to high levels of cultural capital, who often represent welfare institutions or see the traditional role of government as public service, and a senior state nobility, with high levels of economic capital, who speak on behalf of finance and promote market oriented neo-liberal reforms. This conflict figures centrally in a number of Bourdieu's polemical and political interventions.[22] Here, he highlights a conflict – which bears a superficial resemblance to the division between left and right Hegelians[23] – between the 'left hand' and the 'right hand' of the state. The left hand of the state includes functionaries of the state who work in the field of public education, health, social welfare and include social workers, family counsellors, primary and secondary school teachers providing and sustaining public goods and services as representatives of the 'social functions' of the state. They form part of 'the so-called spending ministries which are the trace, within the

---

[22] Bourdieu, Pierre. *Acts of Resistance: Against the Tyranny of the Market*. New York: The New Press, 1999; Bourdieu, Pierre. *Firing Back*. New York, NY: The New Press, 2003; Bourdieu, Pierre. *Political Interventions: Social Science and Political Action*. 2008.

[23] Superficial to the extent that the division between Hegelians was between a left, right, and centre group of Hegelians where a major controversy of the Hegelian inheritance was over the role of religion. See Toews, John. *Hegelianism: The Path Towards Dialectical Humanism, 1805–1841*. Cambridge: Cambridge University Press. 1980.

state, of the social struggles of the past'.[24] Opposed to them are the functionaries of the right hand of the state who follow and champion the logic of the market, favour economic and financial reform and imposie forms of penalty or judicial discipline. This includes 'the technocrats of the Ministry of Finance, the public and private banks and the ministerial cabinets'.[25] The conflict between them centres on finance and spending.

> I think that the left hand of the state has the sense that the right hand no longer knows, or, worse, no longer really wants to know what the left hand does. In any case, it does not want to pay for it. One of the main reasons for all these people's despair is that the state has withdrawn, or is withdrawing, from a number of sectors of social life for which it was previously responsible; social housing, public service.[26]

It is in relation to supporting the left hand of the state, the state conceived in Hegelian and Durkheimian sense, as a state protecting the universal interest or general interest of the population and offering it security, solidarity, freedom and equality in the face of increasing neo-liberalism, that Bourdieu expresses his politics and world-view. He does so in a context where he believes that neo-liberalism is spreading from its North American centre throughout the world via bodies such as the World Bank and the IMF and in which the economy is perceived as a separate domain with its own inviolable natural laws of supply and demand. In these circumstances public services are becoming increasingly privatised and public goods such as health education and culture transformed into commodities to be consumed by clients. Such processes are often rationalised through a trope of individual responsibility. The neo-liberal encroachment of publicly or state-sanctioned private business interests into what were heretofore public-regulated processes such as the regulation of the housing market forms a central theme of *The Social Structures of the Economy* (2004). Neo-liberalism has attempted to demolish the idea of public service, and hastened a retreat and abdication of the social state, whose principal function was to serve the collective interests.

---

[24] Bourdieu, Pierre. *Acts of Resistance*, p. 193.

[25] Ibid., p. 2.

[26] Ibid.

CHAPTER 7

An Assessment of Bourdieu's Theory of the State

Abstract This chapter assesses the value of Bourdieu's theory. It argues that his theory lacks some of the insights found in the work of Elias, Gramsci and Michael Mann. Nevertheless, it argues that Bourdieu provides an original and exciting empirically productive theory of the state when coupled with these other perspectives.

Keywords Elias · Gramsci · Mann · Class · Force · Violence

To recapitulate Bourdieu's argument briefly, the genesis of the state was a recursive phenomenon following the concentration of various capitals – physical, economic, and cultural – around the king and the development of a number of corresponding autonomous social fields, including the cultural, economic and juridical field. But this concentration presupposed and depended upon the prior primitive accumulation of symbolic capital. Within the context of a dynastic state, certain agents of the state, specifically lawyers, made themselves into a state nobility, by instituting the state through a performative discourse regarding what the state was and should be. The vested particular interest of this group, in a weakly autonomous legal field, was to create a discourse based on serving the general interests. It was to provide public service and to enforce universal interests, through the application of law rather than by pursuing personal avarice. Such a mission transcended the interests of agents within the

© The Author(s) 2017
S. Loyal, *Bourdieu's Theory of the State*,
DOI 10.1057/978-1-137-58350-5_7

state, including the king. This process eventually led to the creation of a republic and a nation, independent of the dynastic state:

> I would like to propose . . . that there are a certain number of social agents including lawyers – who played an eminent role, in particular those possessing that capital in terms of organizational resources that was Roman law. These agents gradually built up this thing that we call the state, that is a set of specific resources that authorizes its possessor to say what is good for the social world as a whole, to proclaim the official and to pronounce words that are in fact orders, because they are backed by the force of the official. The constitution of this instance was accompanied by the construction of the state in the sense of population contained within frontiers.[1]

Bourdieu's discussion of the state represents a remarkable development and extension of his overall sociological project. *On the State* contains a dizzying array of insights and fleshes out aspects of the state that have hitherto remained either partial, or at a relatively high level of generality in his other writings. Yet it also raises some problematic concerns a large number of which arise from his construction of the state problematic. As we noted earlier, Bourdieu's analysis is concerned with looking at what the state is, how it functions, and how it emerges but simultaneously with interrogating, through a narrower optic, how the state maintains relations of domination principally through cultural and symbolic rather than physical and material means. Consequently, a large number of what are ordinarily taken as principal dimensions of the state are simply excluded or only discussed in cursory detail. This particularly entails those aspects pertaining to the state dealt with by what Bourdieu pejoratively refers to physical or materialist approaches. Tilly for example had argued:

> The singling out of the organization of armed forces, taxation, policing, the control of food supply, and the formation of technical personnel stresses activities which were difficult, costly and often unwanted by large parts of the population. All were essential to the creation of strong states; all are therefore likely to tell us something important about the conditions under which . . . states come into being.[2]

---

[1] *On the State*, p. 32.

[2] Tilly, *The Formation*, p. 71.

Correspondingly, Bourdieu fails to discuss how state formation is linked to broader social processes, including the development of capitalism and class formation, even though it may be historically prior to such processes.

In this chapter, I will focus on three major lacunae that inhere in Bourdieu's account: firstly, a theoretical vacillation between an omnipotent, encompassing state and a more nuanced, delimited, though neverthless influential state; secondly, the failure to engage with the geo-political, bellicist, and class context of the state; and finally, difficulties that emerge with the polemical nature of his conception of the state.

HOW PENETRATING IS STATE THOUGHT?

Bourdieu, in his account of the state, shifts between a representation of the state as an all-pervasive Leviathan to an articulation of it as one among several delimited, yet powerful, forces shaping the social world. In the former conceptualization the state is everywhere. Underpinning people's activities and social practices are state categories and state classifications that are sanctioned and evaluated through the lexica and criteria of officialdom. This state is an all-seeing, all-supporting architecture of cognition and perception. State thinking appears to be pervasive, ubiquitous and omnipotent: it goes all the way down. The state is akin to Aristotle, Spinoza or Leibniz's god – the unmoved mover or viewpoint of all viewpoints.

This all powerful understanding of the state contrasts with a more prosaic conception of the state. In this gloss state *doxa* is neither completely nor fully internalised by the whoel population. Instead there exists the possibility of creating a cumulative index indicating the disparity between the normative standards held by individuals and those annunciated by the state (Bourdieu, 2014: 36). And even if the state is like a god, not everyone worships the same god-like state, nor to the same degree.

This vacillation in his rendition of the state has been recognised by other writers, though understood in different ways.[3] The manner in which

---

[3] See also Swartz, David. *Symbolic Power, Politics and Intellectuals: the Political Sociology of Pierre Bourdieu*. Chicago: University of Chicago Press, 2013; and Schinkel, Willem 'The Sociologists and the State: An Assessment of Pierre Bourdieu's Sociology' *British Journal of Sociology*, 66(2). 2015, pp. 215–235.

the state is conceptualised has enormous implications for how the social order is maintained, reproduced or resisted by individuals and groups.

Hence, if we adhere to an omnipotent, encompassing view of the state the capacity of social actors to defy the state appears to be severely limited. Such a position yields an interpretation in which social reproduction is viewed as quasi-automatic and social resistance as nigh impossible.

As Bourdieu notes in an interview:

> I think that in terms of symbolic domination, resistance is more difficult, since it is something you absorb like air, something you don't feel pressured by: it is everywhere and nowhere and to escape from that is very difficult ... with the mechanisms of symbolic violence, domination tends to take the form of a more effective, and in this sense more brutal, means of oppression. Consider contemporary societies in which violence has become soft, invisible.[4]

Resistance to imposed beliefs cannot be assumed to come from a 'capacity of consciousness': 'to speak of "ideologies" is to locate in the realm of *representations* – liable to be transformed through this intellectual conversion called "awakening of consciousness" (*prise de conscience*) – what in fact belongs to the order of belief, that is, to the level of the most profound corporeal dispositions'.[5] It is for this reason that Bourdieu criticizes attempts to challenge forms of discrimination such as racism, simply on a discursive level.[6] Such a standpoint begs the question of how social agents can question or resist forms of state thinking? Four major responses appear to be scattered throughout his work. First, on the basis of immanent criticism, states can be denounced and questioned on the basis of the principles of universalisation that they themselves propound. Second, academics can become spokespersons for the dominated arguing for a corporatism of the universal[7] grounded in a *Realpolitik* of reason. Third, as Wacquant notes, 'societies marked by the

---

[4] Bourdieu and Eagleton, p. 270.

[5] Bourdieu, Pierre. *Acts of Resistance: Against the Tyranny of the Market.* New York: The New Press, 1999, pp. 54–55; see also Bourdieu, *Pascalian Meditations,* pp. 164–205.

[6] *Pascalian Meditations,* pp. 180–181.

[7] Bourdieu, Pierre. 'For a Corporatism of the Universal' in Bourdieu, Pierre. *The Rules of Art: Genesis and Structure of the Literary Field.* Cambridge: Polity Press, 1996, pp. 337–348.

proliferation of "situations of maladjustment" between habitus and the world, due to the generalisation of access to education and the spread of social insecurity, offer a fertile terrain for political interventions aimed at fracturing the *doxic* acceptance of the *status quo* and fostering the collective realisation of alternative historical futures'.[8] Fourth, the increasing symbolic efficacy ushered in by complex and lengthy circuits of legitimation can become counterbalanced by the potential for subversive appropriation of the capital tied to one of the multiple, differentiated, hierarchical fields, especially the dominated dominant whose power depends on cultural capital:

> It thus may happen that the interests associated with the dominated positions in the field of cultural production lead to subversive alliances, capable of threatening the social order. This occurs when, in the cognitive struggles over the social world, the professional producers of principles of vision and division, globally located in the dominated positions field of power ... engage their cultural capital in struggles that they more or less completely or more or less durably identify with their own struggles in the field of power.[9]

Contrary to what a number of critics have proposed, Bourdieu is not a deterministic social theorist.[10] Instead, he allots a significant degree of volition to the habitus wherein free action, deriving from the ability to transpose skills to different contexts, stands out against a background of habitual action. What is considered a realisable possibility is a function of skills. Nevertheless, there are, in fact, contradictory tensions permeating Bourdieu's attempt to transcend the divide between the subjective and objective moments in social analysis or what is more commonly refereed to as the agency-structure dichotomy. This tension is re-expressed in his second, more nuanced conception of the state that incorporates social struggles and an increased possibility for social change within its purview.

---

[8] Wacquant, *Bourdieu and Democratic*, p. 20.

[9] *State Nobility*, p. 387.

[10] 'Because the habitus is an endless capacity to engender products –thoughts, perceptions, expressions, actions – whose limits are set by the historically and socially situated conditions of its production, the conditioned and conditional freedom it secures is as remote from a creation of unpredictable novelty as it is from a simple mechanical reproduction of the initial conditionings' *Outline*, p. 95.

His own political interventions express such a vision. In *Acts of Resistance* Bourdieu reminds us that located within the 'left hand' of the state 'are the trace, within the state of the social struggles of the past'[11] and provide the basis for progressive political interventions in the present.

However, this foregrounding of resistance and struggle for the most part remains absent from his all-encompassing, invasive view of the state, and it is this interpretation which tends to predominate in his writings. Here the state is conceived as the creator of logical and moral conformity within which all social actors are, in Thomas Bernard's words, 'servants of the state'.[12] In this understanding, Bourdieu rather hastily shifts from a conception of the state as the creator of logical conformity to that of it as the framer of moral conformity, in effect short-circuiting a relationship that needs to be empirically teased out. Cognitive order does not necessarily beget moral conformity and agreement. As Wittgenstein points out: 'So you are saying that human agreement decides what is true and false?' It is what human beings say that is true and false and they agree on. That is nor agreement in opinions but a form of life.[13] The imposition of state categories and their acceptance not only exaggerates the power of state thinking[14] but also seems to inflate the naturalising function of *doxa*. Not all symbolic forms and values are necessarily internalized and accepted. Individuals may be critical and skeptical of beliefs yet, nevertheless continue to follow them, perhaps for pragmatic reasons or simply out of fear.

Bourdieu's views on social resistance with reference to the imposition of state classifications, categorisations and practices appear embryonic compared to the stress placed upon it by Corrigan and Sayer, for example. They also argue that state forms of thinking are imposed from above, but drawing on E.P. Thompson's work, qualify this by noting that they are experienced in different ways by individuals from below.

By overemphasising a moral and ideological consensus permeating the social world, Bourdieu's position remains susceptible to criticisms made by

---

[11] Bourdieu, Pierre. *Acts of Resistance: Against the Tyranny of the Market*. New York: The New Press, 1999, p. 2. He later adds: 'the state, in every country, is to some extent the trace in reality of social conquests'. Ibid., p. 33.

[12] *Rethinking*, p. 1. For a similar view see also Swartz, *Symbolic Power, Politics and Intellectuals*; and Schinkel, 'The Sociologists and the State'.

[13] Wittgenstein, *Philosophical*, para 241.

[14] Swartz, *Symbolic Power, Politics and Intellectuals*, p. 146.

earlier commentators with regard to his discussion of the operation of a dominant ideology – refered to as the 'dominant ideology thesis'.[15] Simarly it overplays the requirement of states to secure consent or legitimacy from the dominated. Individuals may be critical and skeptical of beliefs yet, nevertheless, continue to follow them, perhaps for pragmatic reasons or out of fear. Assent may be wholly absent. Michael Polanyi, for example, discusses how one individual may exercise a coercive form of power by instilling fear in individuals, without having to gain their consent:

> It is commonly assumed that power cannot be exercised without some voluntary support, as for example by some faithful praetorian guard. I do not think this is true, for it seems that some dictators were feared by everybody; for example, towards the end of his rule, everybody feared Stalin. It is, in fact, easy to see that a single individual might well exercise command over a multitude of men without any appreciable voluntary support on the part of any of them. If in a group of men each believes all the others will obey the commands of a person claiming to be their common superior, all will obey this person as their superior. For each will fear that if he disobeyed him, the others would punish his disobedience at the superior's command, and so all are forced to obey by the mere supposition of the others' continued obedience, without any voluntary support being given to the superior by any member of the group.[16]

Polanyi's may misrepresent the actuality of Stalin's rule but nevertheless indicates an empirical possibility that has implications that are not addressed in Bourdieu's account: that is, of denying a ruler legitimacy, but nevertheless following their dictates. Both Weber and Mosca also recognised this contingency.[17]

---

[15] Bourdieu Pierre and Luc Boltanski. 'La Production de L'Ideologie Dominante' *Actes de la recherche en sciences social*, Juin 3(3). 1976, pp. 4-73; Abercrombie, Hill and Turner. *The Dominant Ideology Thesis*. London: George & Allen Unwin, 1980.

[16] Polyani, Michael. *Personal Knowledge: Towards a Post-Critical Philosophy*. Chicago: University of Chicago Press. 1958, pp. 224–225.

[17] For Mosca how groups were organized was crucial: 'The power of any minority is irresistible as against each single individual in the majority, who stands alone before the totality of the organized minority' Mosca, Gaetano. *The Ruling Class*. New York: MacGraw Hill, p. 53.

A further issue concerning his invasive, rather than delimited, theory of the state centres on whether all thought and categories in the last instance derive from the state. This assertion distances us from a conceptualisation in which the state is embedded within society, where state categorisation interacts or re-configures anterior forms of classification emerging from wider societal contexts or various differentiated forms of life: religious, economic, political or family contexts, for example.[18]

Paradoxically, Durkheim, whose work on the state plays such a prominent role in Bourdieu's own analysis, had given the connection between the state and the wider societal collective conscience it orchestrates, a greater distance:

> It is not accurate to say that the State embodies the collective consciousness, for that goes beyond the state at every point. In the main that consciousness is diffused: there is at all times a vast number of social sentiments and social states of mind (*états*) of all kinds, of which the state hears only a faint echo. The state is the centre only of a particular kind of consciousness, of one that is limited but higher, clearer and with a more vivid sense of itself.[19]

Nevertheless, given the ambivalence he confers on the power of the states, there are times when Bourdieu can also be read as suggesting a position similar to that of Durkheim: that states do not produce or embody all forms of social categorisation but construct some salient forms of categorisation which they attempt to impose upon others already in existence as part of a wider social struggle and to attempt to gain a monopoly in the field of representation. Poupeau claims that Bourdieu's analysis of the state is in fact anchored in his earliest works on Algeria. In those writings Bourdieu discusses the imposition of pre-existing French Metropolian

---

[18] In their analysis of the racialization of legal categories Emigh, Riley and Ahmed attempt to challenge Bourdieu amongst others, by questioning the view that what is considered to be a central feature of state power – the creation of census categories – are actually the product of the state. They argue instead that they are a product of an interaction between state and society. Census categories were already widespread in society before being taken up by the census. Emigh, Rebecca, Ahmed, Patricia, Riley, Dylan, *Changes in Censuses: From Imperialism to Welfare States*. Palgrave Press, 2016.

[19] Durkheim, *Professional Ethics*, pp. 49–50.

bureaucratic categories and structures – in the form of unified territorial units – onto Algerian villages with the result that, in Bourdieu's words, 'geographical proximity predominated over social, genealogical proximity'.[20] Rather than originating in the state, his delimited view of the state allows Bourdieu to be interpreted as arguing that some categories originate with the state while others *ultimately* depend for their force on the authority given to them by the state as the central symbolic authority, the symbolic bank of credit.

This is connected to a further tension in Bourdieu's work: between the notion that the state has a *claim* to the monopoly of symbolic violence, which can be readily accepted, and the assertion that it actually *has* the monopoly of symbolic violence. The latter pronouncement features in *Homo Academicus* where the state is identified as the repository of symbolic violence.[21]

The failure of materialists, including Weber and Elias, to discuss symbolic and legitimation processes in their theory of state formation constitutes the basis for Bourdieu's expanded materialism. Bourdieu rightly argues that all material processes always involve symbolic processes, that is, they are conceptually mediated. However, this ontological argument then appears to become superimposed onto a substantive argument inscribed in his model: that all processes of state formation presuppose some form of prior symbolic accumulation. Symbolic forms are the condition of material forms of domination:

> I believe the primary form of accumulation takes place on the symbolic level. There are people who got themselves obeyed, respected because they are literate, religious, holy, handsome … in other words for heaps of reasons that materialism, in the ordinary sense, does not know what to do with.[22]
> (Bourdieu, 2014: 166–167)

This, however, is an empirical argument and it is not clear whether the initial accumulation of symbolic capital, as the basis of legitimisation, has always historically been a presupposition of other forms of monopolisation and accumulation, including economic accumulation. Such an assertion

---

[20] Poupeau, Franck. 'The Invention of the State: Bourdieu between Bearn and Kabylia' *Berkeley Journal of Sociology*, 159. Dec 2015, p. 9.

[21] Bourdieu, P. *Homo Academicus*, Cambridge: Polity. 1990. p. 27.

[22] *On the State*, pp. 166–167.

also sits uneasily with a more nuanced argument concerning overt physical violence and symbolic violence residing within the same set of social relations found in *Outline of a Theory of Practice.*[23]

The failure to acknowledge the variable acceptance or adherence to beliefs in the strong, invasive view of the state is connected to a further related failing: the variability of state power. This, of course, is also an empirical question. But we require precise yet adjustable tools with which to analyse these substantive processes and to answer questions such as: How wide and variable was the state's reach in different historical periods and across different societies? How widely accepted and penetrating was the state's symbolic power in relation to the population in dynastic states in comparison to modern nation states? What powers and forms of thinking – religious, economic, social etc. – existed outside of the state? In his discussion of earlier forms of state and the emerging modern form of bureaucratic state, Bourdieu, perhaps as an artefact of his condensed description, tends to exaggerate the power and penetration of the state and state thinking viz-a-viz the population as a whole. Effectively, he under-specifies the localised nature and force of customs in social life. For a great deal of their history – seen in a long-term framework of several centuries – have generally been weak in penetrating their populations in this regard.[24] Following on from this, Mann's theoretical framework, which also contains flaws, could nevertheless act as a useful supplement to Bourdieu's own analysis.[25] The concepts of extensive and intensive and authoritative and diffused power are useful tools for looking at the wide variation in state formation and development spanning several centuries and also for examining how extensive the power of the state was in shaping overlapping interactional networks: both historically in emerging European nation states, as well as comparatively under various political regimes. Mann's contrast of infrastructural power that penetrates civil society, and despotic power, wherein the state possesses threadbare means to encroach into civil society, is also sociologically and

---

[23] *Outline.* p. 192).

[24] Mann, Michael, 'States, Ancient and Modern', *Archives Européennes de Sociologie*, 18. 1977; Mann *The Sources of Social Power: Volume 2.*

[25] See for example the various essays in Hall, John and Schroeder, Ralph eds. *An Anatomy of Power: The Social Theory of Michael Mann.* Cambridge: Cambridge University Press, 2006; And Anderson, Perry. 'Michael Mann's sociology of power' in *A Zone of Engagement*, London: Verso. 1992: pp. 76–86.

empirically useful. Both Steinmetz and Jessop have noted that the spatial aspect of state formation – that states' occupy bounded, national territories – is missing from Bourdieu's approach.[26] By contrast, Mann's approach highlights the role of centralised territoriality in terms of foregrounding not just symbolic and cultural forms, but organisation, logistics, communication and technology in state formation within a socio-spatial and organisational model of power.

We have already noted that it is unclear whether Bourdieu, like Durkheim, separates the state from political society. In his essay on the political field, Bourdieu argues that the latter operates in a context in which lay persons delegate their power to professional politicians, attached to a party apparatus, and thereby remove themselves from the instruments of political production. Politicians, in turn, 'represent' these alienated individuals by competing for them as citizens/consumers through the use of opinion polls.[27] This penetrating discussion of delegation and representation, however, remains on the whole analytically separate from his discussion of the state as an arena where the struggle over the distribution of public goods, and as the central bank of symbolic capital conferring authority and backing acts of nomination, takes place. It therefore remains unclear how the two fields are related other than through homology viz-a-viz the field of power? [28] How precisely are the bureaucratic field and the political field articulated.[29] Moreover, the relation between the juridical field and the bureaucratic field equally remains ambiguous. The matrix of legal codes, judicial institutions and specialist personnel is barely mentioned in his discussion of the modern state.[30] To add to the confusion in his historical

---

[26] Steinmetz, George. 'On Bourdieu, Sur l'Etat: Field Theory and the State, Colonies, and Empires' *Sociologica*, 3.2014, p. 1–9; Jessop, Bob. 'The Symbolic Bank of Central Capital: Bourdieu's On the State' *Radical Philosophy*, 193. Sep/Oct. 2015, pp. 33–41.

[27] Bourdieu, *Language*, pp. 171–202.

[28] See also Jessop, *The Central Bank*, p. 39.

[29] Steinmetz who aims to 'use Bourdieu to revise Bourdieu' argues that Bourdieu does not adequately differentiate those who formulate policy from those who implement it, bureaucrats from politicians.

[30] See his penetrating attempt to move beyond instrumentalist and absolute autonomy perspectives on law in Bourdieu, Pierre. 'The Force of Law: Towards a Sociology of the Juridical Field'. *Hastings Law Journal*, 38. 1987, pp. 814–853.

outline of state formation, Bourdieu dissolves the specifics of the legal sphere into a more general discussion of the bureaucratic field, making its subsequent emergence as a semi-autonomous juridical field unclear.

Given this uncertainty in the relations between these core fields, a number of other unresolved questions follow: Does the type of constitution in a state matter? For example, do the distinctions between tyranny, monarchy, democracy, as demarcated by Aristotle,[31] for example, or in modern times between fascism, state socialism, dictatorship or representative democracy affect how we should see and interpret the state? Coincidentally, these were also secondary questions for Durkheim for whom the principal explanatory distinction was between the clear, reflective consciousness of the state and the opaque representations of the masses. And, despite their contemporary importance, they also seem to be marginal concerns for Bourdieu.

In his critical review of Bourdieu theory of the state, Steinmetz has noted that Bourdieu fails to account for a variety of modes of state in his model. This includes: non-European states, colonial states or state forms that possess a markedly different scale, dimension or territorial basis from nation-states, such as Empires which have historically been 'a more typical form of polity than states in world history'.[32]

The ambiguity of symbolic capital

Problems with his materialist theory of the symbolic are attentuated by the widely fluctuating range of reference of his concept of symbolic capital. Given the primary position of symbolic power and the role of the state as a 'central bank of symbolic capital' in setting and determining the relative weight of the other forms of capital, and as both condition for and effect of other capitals, it is clear symbolic capital does a lot of work in his analysis. But its importance is compromised by his shifting definitions of the term. In *Outline of a Theory of Practice*, for example, he gives three different definitions. First, as honour or prestige, that is, its standing in the eyes of other groups. Second, it is how economic and cultural capital appear when they are misrecognised and not perceived as capital, but instead seen through

---

[31] Aristotle. *The Politics*. London: Penguin. 1988, p. 238.
[32] Steinmetz, p. 8.

dominant taxonomies.[33] Finally, symbolic capital is a form of credit.[34] In other places, it refers both to the power of nomination, the ability to impose meanings and classifications as legitimate, the pure form of expression of juridical capital, and to the public recognition that becomes associated with one's capital holdings – whether cultural, economic or social. While, yet in another connected definition in *On the State*, it is integrally tied to political capital.[35] Bourdieu's elastic use of the concept has of course partly to be seen as a result of the dynamic, multiple applications of the term to different empirical contexts and therefore results from the rich empirical studies he undertakes. But this does not justify the enlarged and contradictory theoretical burden he places upon it. The difficulty, as Thompson has also noted in his critique,[36] partly stems from the grammar of the concept of 'recognition' associated with symbolic capital. It can be argued that recognition can mean (1) to recall and remember, to (2) to perceive or understand, (3) to honour and value or (4) to acknowledge and accept. Bourdieu's discussion seems to presuppose all four multivalent definitions often shifting between them.

MOVING BEYOND EXISTING APPROACHES OF THE STATE

It was noted above that Bourdieu's *On the State* engages with a number of classical and contemporary analyses of the state which he uses as either a basis upon, or sounding board against, he constructs his own model of the state. In particular, it conjoins the Durkheimian view of the state – as the social organ through which the collective conscience of a social order is regulated – with the Weberian discussion of the state that possesses a

---

[33] 'Symbolic capital a transformed and thereby *disguised* form of physical "economic" capital, produces its own proper effect inasmuch, and only inasmuch, as it conceals the fact that it originates in "material" forms of capital which are also, in the last analysis, the source of its effects Bourdieu, *Outline*, p. 183.

[34] 'Once one realizes that symbolic capital is always credit, in the widest sense of the word, i.e., a sort of advance which the group alone can grant those who give it the best material and symbolic guarantees, it can be seen that the exhibition of symbolic capital (which is always very expensive in economic terms) is one of the mechanisms which (no doubt universally) make capital go to capital. Ibid., p. 181.

[35] Bourdieu, *On the State*, 2014, p. 192.

[36] Thompson, J. *Studies in the Theory of Ideology*. Cambridge: Polity Press, 1984, pp. 59–60.

monopoly of physical violence and secures legitimation. But his definition also engages to a greater and lesser extent with a number of modern social thinkers who are criticized for ignoring the symbolic aspect of the state. It may therefore be useful to examine his view of the state by comparing his position with just two of them: Norbert Elias, who is generally reviewed favourably and who shares a similar political world-view, but is nevertheless criticized, and Antonio Gramsci whose work is summarily dismissed. Both theorists reveal problems with Bourdieu's approach and undermine his claim that his analysis of the state has superseded theirs. Their theories demonstrate that his understanding of the state remains one-sided especially when it comes to undertaking a broad range of empirical, historical and comparative forms of enquiry into multi-dimensional state forms that vary across the globe.

That Bourdieu and Elias shared a mutual respect for each other's work which can be seen in their correspondence.[37] Parallels between their sociological theories have also been recognised by a number of authors.[38] However, their overlapping conceptual vocabulary and similar attention to the social, relational and historical nature of social forms may camouflage the divergences between their respective sociological visions, especially in relation to the state.

Elias's approach to the state and state formation is not without problems, and Bourdieu pinpoints some of its limitations. But there are several respects in which Elias's account of state and state formation remains superior to Bourdieu's own account, and could usefully act as a supplement to it. First, Elias is more cautious about applying terms such as political, economic or ideological (symbolic) in a causal sense,[39] as Bourdieu tends to do in his general sociology. Not only because these terms cannot be applied to undifferentiated feudal social relations, as Bourdieu recognises, but also because

---

[37] Elias. *Elias & Bourdieu Correspondence*. Deutsches Literaturarchiv Marbach and Neckar, 1987.

[38] Chartier, Roger. *The Sociologist and the Historian*, Cambridge: Polity, 2015; Dunning, Eric and Hughes, Jason. *Norbert Elias and Modern Sociology*, London: Bloomsbury. 2013.

[39] For Elias causality is often more complex, in terms of the reciprocity between cause and effect, and sometimes the term cause needs to be replaced by concept of correspondence. State formation, the increase in division of labour, in the length of chains of interdependence, the growth of towns, trade and money, and the growth of an administrative apparatus are reinforcing processes with no causal priority.

they are abstractions which look at the same nexus of social relations or figurations, from different points of view. An economic sphere or field also retains a symbolic and political aspect. By contrast, Bourdieu's discussion of economic, cultural, political fields and their attendant forms of capital can sometimes map onto what Elias calls 'spherical thinking'.[40] Second, Elias tends to be more reflexive than Bourdieu in terms of his use of 'processual concepts' that take account of, and try to capture, various social balances and power ratios pertaining to figurations. Elias rarely talks about monopolisation *per se* but rather *high degrees* of monopolisation of violence and taxation. The emphasis is on shifts in power balances between groups and social relations, not on absolutes. Although Bourdieu, at one point for example, uses the term 'statization', or acknowledges the existence of 'relatively' public monopolies,[41] his discussion of the move from the personal rule of dynastic kings to the impersonal rule of the bureaucratic state, or from the private to the public, predominantly uses hard-edged contrasts and binaries, deriving ultimately from structuralism. Binaries are of course useful in creating contrasts within social forms, and they are the stock in trade of sociology – *gemeinschaft-gesellschaft*, status-contract, military-industrial, feudalism-capitalism etc. – but they are less effective in capturing empirical continuities and contradictory multi-polar tendencies and ambivalences. Third, Elias's approach is more systematic and methodologically comparative in respect of looking at France, Germany and England. Bourdieu, also looks at these countries in addition to Japan and China, particularly in his lectures in *On the State*, but this is undertaken more impressionistically, and with less comparative rigour. Bourdieu's primary scientific methodological heuristic is based upon the construction of a 'model' which, although drawn from the French epistemological tradition including Canguilhem, Koyre and Bachelard, has strong affinities with Weber's ideal types as well as Hegel's notion of the Concept. Instead, and despite his discussions of other countries, Bourdieu's view of the state appears to take the pre- and post-revolutionary French state as paradigmatic as other commentators have also recognised.[42] Still others have also highlighted the problem of using Prussia or France, peculiarly centralised

[40] Elias, Norbert, *What is Sociology.* London: Hutchinson. 1970.

[41] *On the State*, p. 130.

[42] Scott, Alan. 'We are the State. Pierre Bourdieu and the Political Field' *Rivista di Storia delle Idee* 2.1 2013, pp. 65–70; Jessop, *On the State*.

states, as their model of the state.[43] Bourdieu's ruminations on the notions of 'public service', 'public good', 'public interest' and disinterestedness which all stem from his lectures at the *Collège de France* delivered immediately prior to those contained in *On the State,* are largely specific to the French bureaucratic state. Such a state may, however, historically be more of an exception rather than rule in terms of its centralisation, reach and penetration of its population. Marx, for example, had famously discussed its highly bureaucratised nature in the *Eighteenth Brumaire* as far back as the 1850s:

> It is immediately obvious that in a country like France, where the executive power commands an army of officials numbering more than half a million individuals and therefore constantly maintains an immense mass of interests and livelihoods in the most absolute dependence; where the state enmeshes, controls, regulates, superintends, and tutors civil society from its most comprehensive manifestations of life down to its most insignificant stirrings, from its most general modes of being to the private existence of individuals; where through the most extraordinary centralization this parasitic body acquires a ubiquity, an omniscience, a capacity for accelerated mobility, and an elasticity which finds a counterpart only in the helpless dependence, the loose shapelessness of the actual body politic.[44]

In this sense, despite his reflexive exclamations to the contrary, Bourdieu's thought remains trapped in a national form of sociology. Fourth, Elias gives greater importance to the international or the geo-political context within which the national state is enmeshed, and attempts, through his concept of figurations, to look *simultaneously* at how changes in inter-state processes reciprocally impact upon changes in intra-state processes. As Hintze (1975: 183) noted long ago, it was the 'external ordering of the states' and their 'overall position in the world which was central to understanding state organisation'.[45] An international dimension, however, is largely absent in Bourdieu's conceptualisation acquiring barely more than two pages of discussion in *On the State.* Consequently, his discussion of state formation is almost wholly 'internalist' – examining the inner logic

---

[43] Morgan and Orloff, *The Many Hands,* p. 7.

[44] Marx, *The Eighteenth Brumaire,* p. 186.

[45] Hintze, Otto. *The Historical essays of Otto Hintze.* New York: Oxford University Press, 1975, p. 183.

and conflicts within a country centred on strategies of reproduction and their concomitant mechanisms. A higher level of synthesis, in which interdependent inter-state actions have unplanned consequences for intra-state actions, is thereby ommitted. This points to a fifth connected virtue of Elias's work – his commitment to understanding the role of war and violence in state formation. That war is a central component of state formation is not peculiar to Elias but was also, of course, a central theme in Hintze and Weber's work as well as neo-Weberian and modern accounts of state formation.[46] In relation to such 'bellicist' readings of the state, Bourdieu definition of the state as having both a monopoly of *physical and* symbolic violence needs to be acknowledged. In addition, he briefly discusses the emergence of a military and police force in the formation of military capital. Compared to his discussion of symbolic and cultural processes, however, these are relegated to peripheral concerns. For Elias, by contrast, force, violence and war play a fundamental role in state-formation. Focusing on how increasing internal pacification within a territory was connected with increasing and bigger wars abroad, especially against neighbouring territories, helps us to see that European state formation consisted of a realm of warring states who had to adapt to this competition by centralising political power and collecting taxes to fund wars. As Hobson, discussing Elias, notes:

> Important here is that the costs of military technology under conditions of inter-feudal war increased at the same time that new forms of warfare – especially the rise of the mercenary army and later the professional standing army – shifted the opportunity structure for successful state-centralisation... the ontological primacy of international anarchy recalibrates the ontological status of state-society relations into that of an intervening variable. Moreover, in this vision the state becomes reconfigured around its capacity to be adaptive to the logic of international anarchy.[47]

Tilly, whose work Bourdieu also dismisses as part of a 'physicalist theory' in addition to its pronounced economism,[48] also rightly foregrounded

---

[46] Hinzte especially made this central: 'All state organization was originally military organization for war'. 1975: Hintze, *The Historical Essays*, p. 181.

[47] Hobson, John. *Human Figurations*, vol 1, 2. 2012.

[48] *On The State*, p. 135.

coercion and war, arguing that 'war makes states': 'War wove the European network of national states, and preparation for war created the internal structures of the state within it'.[49] Changes in war technology, the use of mercenary and then a professional standing army, and its increased financial costs were all major factors shaping states, as were increasing demands from citizens in response. For Tilly war required not only increased taxation, but also expanding credit.[50]

Given this apparent analytical consensus it may then seem odd that Bourdieu discounts the role of physical force while emphasising the constitutive role of symbolic and cultural forms in his discussion of statehood. It has often been noted that Bourdieu is fond of 'pushing the stick in the opposite direction'.[51] But at a deeper level, his privileging of culture and symbolic domination over coercion and violence reflects his underlying philosophical anthropology based on 'recognition and misrecognition', i.e. the notion that to be, is to be perceived.[52] A final aspect in which Elias's theory of state formation supersedes Bourdieu's is in terms of another contextual variable – Elias's stronger focus on class. Elias's book the *Civilizing Process* is subtitled 'Changes in the Behaviour of the Secular Upper-Class in the West' and is centrally concerned with the conflict and contestation between the descending nobility and rising bourgeoisie. Elias was conscious of class fractions, for example, the division in the bourgeoisie between administrators who generally supported the *ancien regime* and wished to acquire the rights and entitlements of the nobility, and the enterprising merchant part of the bourgeoisie who were more inclined to challenge the *status quo*. But he was also acutely aware of the ambivalence inherent in any such conflict. For such a merchant, any challenge to the monarch might potentially destabilise the entire social order, threatening their own intermediary position within it. For Elias, it is not symbolic domination *per se*, but the overall structure of the configuration and the interests of the groups within it, that compels them to act in certain ways.

---

[49] Tilly, *Capital, Coercion*, p. 76.

[50] Ibid., p. 95.

[51] Morgan, K. and a. Orloff. 'The Many Hands of the State', p. 19.

[52] Bourdieu, *Pascalian Meditations*, pp. 238–245; *On the State*, 192; Wacquant, 'Pierre Bourdieu' in Rob Stones (ed.) *Key Sociological Thinkers*, London: Palgrave, p. 265.

This is neither a question of the nobility being free or forced but a question of the variable degrees of compulsion operating upon them in a given conjuncture of interdependencies.

Against Gramsci

Bourdieu's omission of any discussion of class conflict entailed in state formation, and a disinclination to recognise broader social processes including the development of capitalism and class formation, convieniently takes us into Gramsci's discussion of the state. Unlike Elias, who though criticized is nevertheless recognised for his pioneering insights, Gramsci is dismissed in the most derogatory and off-hand way: 'Much could be said about Gramsci as the Ptolemy of the Marxist system, who gave the appearance of a path of rescue from the system while hemming people even more into this blind alley'.[53] Despite this criticism, there are nonetheless parallels and divergences in their theoretical approaches to the state. In *On the State*, Bourdieu had suggested dissolving the distinction between the state and civil society to look instead, in a Durkheimian manner, at the continuum of access for individuals to collective resources and their adherence to state cultural values. The civil-society /state binary, although often assumed to be foundational for Hegelian and Marxist theories of the state, is actually also dissolved in the Hegelian approach. Given Hegel's notion of sublation, *aufhebung*, civil society (as well as the family) is both negated, preserved, and 'lifted up' within the moment of the state: the dichotomy between civil society and state therefore is not an absolute one. This blurring of boundaries is something Gramsci, under the influence of Croce, also grappled with through his concept of the 'integral state'. Retaining though modifying the concept of civil society in which a war of position takes place, Gramsci conceives of civil society as penetrated by, yet also partially independent from the state, as a central arena of social struggles. Such a conception allows Gramsci to investigate the possibility of social resistance to the state and state ideology, in a way largely, though not completely, absent in Bourdieu's discussion. Gramsci's concept of counter-hegemony[54] hinging on a discussion of intellectual and moral

---

[53] *On the State*, p. 141.

[54] Gramsci, Antonio. *Selections from the Prison Notebooks*. London: Lawrence and Wishart. 1971, p. 333.

reform, contradictory consciousness and common sense, plays a fundamental explanatory role here. Elias's insight as to the ambivalence present in all power relationships, is mirrored in Gramsci's reading of social formations in which deference and rebellion can be seen to reside and alternate within the same individual, evoked by the contingencies of particular contexts, social situations or events. E. P. Thompson elaborates

> "two theoretical consciousnesses" can be seen as derivative from two aspects of the same reality: on the one hand, the necessary conformity with the *status quo* if one is to survive, the need to get by in the world as it is in fact ordered, and to play the game according to the rules imposed by employers, overseers of the poor, etc.; on the other hand the "common sense" derived from shared experience with fellow workers and with neighbours of exploitation, hardship and repression, which continually exposes the text of the paternalist theatre to ironic criticism and (less frequently) to revolt.[55]

The picture of individuals divided by adherence to social values while simultaneously retaining a feeling of revolt against them, paints a more complex picture than Bourdieu allows in his view of symbolic violence and the internalisation of *doxa*. The concept of contradictory consciousness would of course be anathema to Bourdieu, who stresses instead the practical and unconscious nature of our acceptance of social hierarchies. Gramsci does, however, attempt to embed his notion within a theory of action and praxis.[56] He also explores the extent to which ideologies or dominant belief systems need not be opposed in their totality, but maybe amenable to transformation through the preservation and rearrangement of their most durable elements. Such a view also belies Bourdieu's crude characterisation of Marxist theories of ideology as presupposing a Cartesian view of the individual, and a simple 'reflection theory' of consciousness. This may ring true of Lenin and the Second International, but it caricatures many modern Marxist positions, which frequently recognise (to use Austin's terms) both the constative and performative role of

[55] Thompson, Edward Palmer. 1991. *Customs in Common*. London: Penguin, p. 11.

[56] A person's two consciousnesses: 'one which is implicit in his activity and which in reality unites him with all his fellow workers in the practical transformation of the real world; and one, superficially explicit or verbal, which he has inherited from the past and uncritically absorbed. Gramsci, *Selections*, p. 333.

language and beliefs.[57] The role of ideology in Marxist and post-Marxist analyses is often discussed in a more nuanced manner than Bourdieu's reductive condemnation suggests.[58]

Significantly, Gramsci also explores the critical the relationship between coercion/violence and symbolic domination/consent at another level of abstraction. Bourdieu, as we have noted, had either ignored the importance of force or blurred the boundaries of this and the symbolic realm by examining communication as a form of force and violence, while still retaining the notion of physical force or what he calls 'raw power'[59] which was nevertheless always accompanied by a symbolic effect. But although this can be acknowledged at one level, such a suggestion downplays the significance of physical violence as an autonomous force in social life, albeit symbolically accompanied and mediated. For Gramsci, by contrast, the acquisition of consent is usually only feasible when there is also physical force to back it up, and the exercise of this force often depends 'on the consent of the majority'.[60]

Moreover, Bourdieu's etymological use of the term 'violence' stretches the 'grammar of the concept' to its comprehensible limit whilst simultaneously downplaying the significance of physical violence as a substantive and independent force in its own right, albeit symbolically accompanied and mediated.[61] Again, an Eliasian account of differential tilts and balances would perhaps be more useful here. Hence, it may be fruitful to retain a sharp distinction between the concepts of force and consent – albeit recognising these concepts are both symbolically and materially mediated – whilst examining empirical shifts in their balance. Gramsci, of course, does this through the concept of hegemony as the organisation of consent. To similar effect, Elias explored the shifting balance between external constraints *(Fremdzwange)* and internalised self-constraints *(Selbstzwange)* as a central dimension of the process of civilisation.[62]

---

[57] Austin, *How to Do Things.*

[58] See for example, Eagleton, Terry. *Ideology: An Introduction*, London: Verso, 1991.

[59] *The State Nobility*, p. 383.

[60] Gramsci *Selections*, p. 80.

[61] See especially Poggi, *The State, its nature, and development,*1990.

[62] Elias, *Civilizing Process*, pp. 365, 378.

Furthermore, the kind of social consensus generated within society that Bourdieu attributes to the power of state schooling and symbolic violence may be more usefully interpreted through a Gramscian optic, as the hegemonic outcome of the power of universal suffrage and representative democracy. As Riley argues it is democracy that brings legitimacy and stability to modern states rather than the symbolic violence of state and school processes.

Unlike Gramsci, Bourdieu rarely discusses the role of democracy in reproducing the social order in his work. However, he does hint at a similar view especially when discussing the related concept of 'parliamentarization'. Parliament, he argues in passing, is a co-condition for the production of the citizen along with the constitution of the state as a juridically governed territory providing rights and duties. It functions as a site of regulated consensus or 'dissension within limits' that helps perpetuate those regimes called democratic.[63] In this discussion of the political field, Bourdieu also points to the individualisation democracy enforces in relation to the collectivity, especially in terms of the political alienation the most dominated groups experience viz-a-viz professional politicians who monopolize access to political instruments.[64] Despite these insights, he primarily views *doxic* adhesion arising from state schooling as generating consensus in the social world.

It is often overlooked that Weber had defined the secular power of the state's monopoly of force in conjunction with and distinction to the 'hierocratic' spiritual domination and monopoly of the church: 'which enforces its order through psychic coercion by distributing or denying religious benefits ("hierocratic coercion")'.[65] By insisting that the school has usurped the symbolic role formerly played by religion Bourdieu fails to

---

[63] *On the State*, p. 355.

[64] 'The silence that weighs on the conditions which force citizens, all the more brutally the economically and culturally deprived they are, to face the alternative of having to abdicate their rights by abstaining from voting or being dispossessed by the fact that they delegate power' Bourdieu, *Language and Symbolic Power*. p. 171. Democratic processes can also be read within Bourdieu's framework as a means of establishing *doxa*. There have been several applications of his work to understand democratic politics see the contributions in Wacquant, *Pierre Bourdieu and Democratic Politics*.

[65] Weber, *Economy and Society*, p. 54.

acknowledge the enduring impact of religious forms and their continuing role in effecting symbolic domination.

As already noted, although Bourdieu explores at length the dynamics of class reproduction in institutions such as schools, he eschews almost entirely the role of class in relation to state formation. When class struggle does appear in Bourdieu's analysis of the state, as for example in the *State Nobility*, it is in terms of the struggles within the dominant rather than between the dominant and dominated. Of course one does not need to endorse E.P. Thompson or Raphael Samuel's view of history from below. Rather you need to understand such processes from both ends: above and below.

He is certainly not obliged to take up the subject, and rightly wary of applying the language of class with thoroughly modern referents to social estates that existed in the completely different social and cultural order of Medieval Europe. Hence the *noblesse de robe* are seen as a status group rather than a class: their major function is seen in terms of their universalising role, albeit for their own particular interests.[66] But one can recognise the fundamental difference between classes in modern capitalist social orders and those in feudal society, as Marx did, yet acknowledge that class and the dynamics of exploitation nevertheless also plays a constitutive and explanatory role in earlier formations. This is especially the case with respect to the class conflict between lords and peasants during the feudal era, which provides a backdrop against which Bourdieu's discussion of the dynastic state takes place. In addition to international relations and war, the role of class conflict, capitalism and exploitation need to have a more prominent role in Bourdieu's analysis of state formation. This means that the contradictory reproduction strategies that Bourdieu emphasises as the motor underpinning state formation – between family and educational reproduction – need to be embedded in the wider class context of property relations between landlords and peasants entailing the extraction of labour

---

[66] Bourdieu may be justified in not using the term class in the twentieth or thirteenth century but is he also in the seventeenth or twentieth when he still sees the state nobility as a status group. Is not their class condition, as for example in Goldmann's *The Hidden God*, where Jansenism, Pascal's and Racine's tragic disposition to the world are outlined of some importance? Goldmann, Lucien. *The Hidden God: A study of Tragic Vision in the Pensees of Psacal and the Tragedies of Racine*. London: Routledge & Kegan Paul, 1964.

services or feudal rent. As Riley, drawing on the work of Brenner, shrewdly observes in his critique of Bourdieu's analysis of the state:

> Monarchs had to get land to provide for excess members of their household. But the search for land of the second son was itself linked to a broader system of social property relations that Bourdieu does not explain at all ... Prior to some time after the fifteenth century in England, agricultural productivity was very low. The reason for this is fairly well known. Although lords owned land, they had little ability or incentive to improve productive processes that were effectively under the control of the main direct producers: the peasantry. This is the fundamental context within which impartable inheritance, the main family strategy Bourdieu emphasizes, could produce zero-sum conflicts within dynastic families.[67]

It was the scarcity of land and the productivity it yielded that engendered marriage strategies and war. The class conflict between lords and peasants also impacted upon levels of taxation and the formation of a centralised bureaucracy distributing these rents to the nobility. Bourdieu's omission of class may be for a number of reasons. Firstly, as he states himself, he is reacting against reductionist Marxist analyses of the state where a crude, functionalist class analysis provides a ubiquitous and sometimes the only theoretical lens. Second, Bourdieu has his own distinctive analysis of 'what makes a social class?'[68] which by-passing discussions of exploitation, fuses the performative power of language with Marx's distinction between a class in itself and for itself and Sartre's distinction between series and a fused group. However, a major reason for his exclusion of class analysis, and his general animosity towards the Marxist position on the state, is probably the polemical nature of his writing on the state and his political worldview – as a left Republican or radical social democrat. This entails a perspective on the nature of the state and its capabilities that diverges in marked respects from Marxist accounts. Bourdieu rarely reads Marx or Marxists on the state with a 'principle of charity', even though aspects of Marx's thinking has had considerable effect in shaping his overall work. This antagonism towards Marxist writers not only includes Gramsci but

---

[67] Riley, *The New Durkheimianism*, p. 272.

[68] Bourdieu, P. 'What Makes a Social Class? On the Theoretical and Practical Existence of Groups', *Berkeley Journal of Sociology* 32(1). 1987, pp. 1–18.

also others such as Perry Anderson, whose important, two-volume work is dismissed as 'a pretentious redefinition of what historians. have already said, on the basis of historical propositions taken second-hand'.[69] The vigour and rancour of his critique reveals the polemical nature of his approach. Bourdieu's work on the state then has to be read simultaneously as theoretical and a political intervention confronting both an ascendant neo-liberalism on the right, and Marxism on the far left.

DURKHEIM AND HEGEL CONTRA MARX

It was noted in the introduction that Bourdieu's writings on the state emerged in the mid-1980s to confront a range of intellectual and socio-economic political problems facing France at the time. In accord with his long-standing Durkheimian inspired Republican – socialist political world-view and his Hegelian philosophical anthropology centred on recognition, it is to Durkheim and Hegel's theories of the state that Bourdieu turns, albeit critically, in order to garner central aspects of the form and content of his model of the state. Through a critical allying of the Durkheimian and Hegelian tradition, a Janus faced state imbricated in social domination on the one hand, simultaneously and ideally embodies and represents the general or universal will on the other. It does this by curbing the destructive forces of unregulated markets while maintaining and fostering the freedom of the individual.

The intellectual background to his lectures at the *Collège de France* collected in *On the State* shed further light on their Hegelian content and intent. In the two years immediately prior, Bourdieu had given lectures on the constitution of the juridical and bureaucratic field, and on public service, public good and disinterestedness.[70] In the second of these set of lectures, he argued that the state maintained its domination and power by claiming to act as a representative of the universal interest, that is, by claiming an interest in disinterestedness. Briefly stated, Bourdieu is engaging with the Hegelian analysis of the state, the *Idea* of the state especially in its ethical moment, as the unity of subjective consciousness and objective order, and of the state bureaucracy as the universal class, acting for society's general interest. Such a view also has striking similarities

---

[69] *On the State*, p. 78.
[70] Champagne et al., p. 379.

with Durkheim's analysis of the state. Although Bourdieu rarely mentions Hegel,[71] aspects of the latter's system nevertheless furnish fundamental constituents in his own discussion of the state. Hegel, when discussing the unity of subject and state in terms of consciousness, had famously remarked that

> But habit blinds us to that on which our whole existence depends. When we walk the streets at night in safety, it does not strike us that this might be otherwise. The habit of feeling safe has become second nature, and we do not reflect on just how this is due solely to the working of special institutions. Commonplace thinking often has the impression that force holds the state together, but in fact its only bond is the fundamental sense of order which everybody possesses.[72]

In the *Philosophy of Right* (1991[1821]), Hegel had conceived the state as the realisation of the Idea of *Sittlichkeit:* as the articulation of freedom and reason. Arguing for the subsumption of the particularity of the family and civil society, abstract expressions of *Sittlichkeit* under the more concrete universality of the state bureaucracy, the *Beamenstaat*, was conceived as a manifestation of the state Idea. The universal class of civil servants served as a crucial mediating link between the particularism of civil society and the universalism of state in maintaining subjective and objective freedom, taking a role as Avineri perceptively points out, akin to Plato's Guardians.[73] Appointed on the basis of meritocracy, knowledge and ability, rather than

---

[71] However, he does note this in his book, *The State Nobility*: '(nearly as positively disposed towards the idealized vision that the state nobility has of itself as a "universal class" as Hegel', *The State Nobility*, p. 376; and 'While technocrats, as unwitting Hegelians, spontaneously lay claim to the privileges of the "universal class"' Ibid., p. 382.

[72] Hegel, George. 1821. *The Philosophy of Right*, trans. and notes by TM Knox, Oxford, Oxford University Press, 1971. p. 282. Hegel adds: 'The state is mind fully mature and it exhibits its moments in the daylight of consciousness'. Ibid., p. 283.

[73] Aveneri, Shlomo, *Hegel's Theory of the State*. Cambridge: Cambridge University Press. 1972, p. 158.

through venality of office, the bureaucracy could carry out its role of being 'dispassionate, upright, and polite'[74] on a materialist criterion – that the state would provide it fixed tenure and pay its wages so as to insulate it from the interests of private property. In order to do this, the bureaucracy had to be perceived by citizens in civil society as disinterested. A central function of this bureaucracy was to tame and regulate egoistic desires, the self-interested actions of individuals where each treated the other as a means to an end – rather than a Kantian end in itself – and to counter balance the competition and subjective freedoms rampant and fostered by *bürgerliche Gesellschaft*. For Hegel, laissez-faire 'a wild beast that needs a constant and strict taming and mastery'[75] was, as is neo-liberalism for Bourdieu, untenable leading not only to the fragmentation of social life but also to extremes of wealth and poverty, which were destabilising for society. As an idea in the minds of the citizens, individuals become bonded to the unity in difference of the state not through sentiment, virtue or from an act of benevolent sacrifice, but through rational reflection: an awareness that their participation in public life was in their own self-interest. Bourdieu's view of the state is, of course, not identical to Hegel's who in addition to a universal class, championed a constitutional monarchy and an elitism that excluded the vast mass of labourers. Rather it shares a number of family resemblances with it – especially the notions of the state as Idea, of participation in the state based upon self interest, and the universalism of the state bureaucracy; but it is also critical of Hegel's characterisation of a homogenous bureaucracy.

Hegel's impact on Bourdieu's philosophical anthropology based on recognition was evident from his earliest work on Algeria. His influence re-emerges, however, in a new political conjuncture in French history following a major shift in political co-ordinates from the time of the Algerian war. Now in a time of ascending neo-liberalism, Bourdieu draws upon Hegel's theory of the state entailing a bureaucracy that stands above sectional interests. We have noted already that Bourdieu draws heavily on Durkheim's theory of the state but this is

---

[74] Hegel, *Philosophy of Right*, p. 193.
[75] Cited in Beiser, Frederick. *Hegel*, London: Routledge, 2005. p. 249.

conjoined with Hegel's analysis of the state, which Bourdieu sees as sharing many similar characteristics.[76] Although Bourdieu does not discuss, let alone enumerate these, they include: their joint focus on corporations as mediating the relation between individual and the state; the moral dimension of the state built around the free rational individual; of the state as an organic whole, a larger life greater and above the individual wills that compose it; of the unifying role of patriotism; of the beneficial aspects of increasing social division of labour; finally of Durkheim's view of the state as serving the 'general interest', and Hegel's belief that it represents the 'universal interest'. As was the case with Durkheim, Bourdieu does not make his indebtedness to Hegel explicit.

Bourdieu like Hegel, identifies the role of the official as one of disinterestedness and acting on behalf of the public, the universal interest of society, and not for his or her private interests. But he then adds a Weberian twist to Hegel's argument: an interest in the *universal*, in impartiality and social justice as an end, is used by the bureaucracy in its official representations of itself, to serve its *particular* interest. By speaking in the name of the public good, and defining the public good, through publicly accepted language, of the universal, of the social whole – as did legal prophets formerly for Weber – such officials simultaneously appropriate for themselves a particular resource that is seen as a universal resource. The idea of acting for the public, for the universal, however, is an ambivalent process. On the one hand, it creates an impression of acting according to universal values in numerous social spheres based on reason, virtue and conforming to laws which benefit the general population; but on the other, it is motivated by particular group self-interests whose actions are often based more on appearance than substance. Nevertheless, the overall unintended effect is a general diffusion of public and universal values throughout society. This, then is Bourdieu's less metaphysical version of Hegel's notion of the 'cunning of reason' – *List der Vernunft* – itself combining Smith's conception of an 'invisible hand' and Kant's *Idea for a Universal Cosmopolitan Reason* – where for Hegel the pursuit of self-interest by individuals within civil society and expanding division of labour ultimately is to the benefit of individuals as a whole,

---

[76] Wacquant and Bourdieu, *From Ruling,* p. 40.

as historical reason unveils itself behind people's backs' so to speak. Bourdieu expresses it thus:

> The universal is the object of universal recognition and the sacrifice of selfish (especially economic) interests is universally recognized as legitimate . . . This means that all social universes tend to offer, to varying degrees, material or symbolic profits of universalization (those very profits pursued by strategies seeking to 'play by the rule'). It also implies that the universes which, like the bureaucratic field, demand with utmost insistence that one submits to the universal, are particularly favourable to obtaining such profits . . . The profit of universalisation is no doubt one of the historical engines of the progress of the universal. This is because it favours the creation of universes where universal values (reason virtue, etc.) are at least verbally recognized and wherein operates a circular process of mutual reinforcement of the strategies of universalization seeking to obtain the profits (if only negative) associated with conformity to universal rules and to the structure of those universes officially devoted to the universal.[77]

Hence, even though the appearance of disinterestedness, acting for the public good as a whole or for the universal, is regularly contradicted in practice by bureaucratic corruption, not only in nascent dynastic states but even in modern France,[78] in the long term the forces pushing for public service nevertheless increase the importance of the universal and general interest of society. The use of the language of the universal by bureaucrats for their own particular interests, entrap them within parameters of action delimited by universal interests. The universal class of bureaucrats are 'obliged to invoke the universal in order to exercise their domination, and they cannot avoid being caught up in their own game and having to subject their practice to norms with claims to universality'.[79]

This is part of the ambiguity or Janus faced nature of the state which, according to Bourdieu, Marxists overlook. The double reality of the state conjoining domination and integration, monopolisation and unification,

---

[77] Bourdieu, *Rethinking*, p. 17.

[78] Bourdieu, Pierre, *Political Interventions: Social Science and Political Action*. p. 197.

[79] Bourdieu, *The State Nobility*, pp. 382–383.

punitiveness and progression is neglected at the expense of a simple-minded Marxist condemnation of its existence.

In *On the State* (2014), Bourdieu's discussion of the bureaucracy as a universal class is therefore partly filtered through Marx's critique of Hegel, and Weber's discussion of legal bureaucratic domination. Marx criticized Hegel not only for beginning with an abstraction, the state idea, but also by arguing that the state bureaucracy defends particular interests, ultimately those of property. He also criticized Hegel's failure to acknowledge that members of the bureaucracy would-view themselves as 'owning the state', though Hegel did in fact recognise this.[80] Bourdieu's discussion on the bureaucracy appears to constitute a half-way house between Hegel and Marx's analyses, but it is clearly more indebted to Hegel. This assertion, however, needs to be qualified. By contrast to Hegel, Bourdieu conceives the bureaucracy as part of a fractured field divided between a higher state nobility representing the right-hand of the state and a lower state nobility standing for the left-hand. Bureaucrats remain entrenched in an endemic conflict to impose their vision of the world and in competition to simultaneously determine the stakes of the struggle. For Bourdieu, Hegel with his concept of the universal will, and Durkheim with his Rousseauian concept of the general will – while rightly emphasising the idealistic or cognitive nature of the state – have often taken up the idealised vision that the state nobility has of itself. Durkheim, moreover, had identified the progress of society with increasing division of labour and integration, but he neglected the fact that integration was simultaneously a precondition of domination. Bourdieu is, therefore, critical of both Hegel and Durkheim but also, at the end of the day, an advocate of their position on the state in terms of their Republican belief that the state – more specifically what he refers to as its left hand – ultimately both needs to and has the political efficacy and power to regulate the market and protect human freedom for the collective good of society. It is, to use Cassirer's distinction, to become a rational state rather than a mythical state.[81] The neo-liberal encroachment of publicly or state-sanctioned private business interests into what were

---

[80] See Hegel, 1971 para 294. However, Hegel felt these interests would be checked by the multiplicity of corporations and voluntary organizations.

[81] Cassier, Ernst. *The Myth of the State*, Yale: Yale University Press, 1946.

heretofore public-regulated processes such as the regulation of the housing market is a central theme of *The Social Structures of the Economy* (2004). For Bourdieu, as for Hegel (and Durkheim), the drive to dissolution of an unregulated economy based on uncontrolled growth, individual responsibility and greed needs to be subordinated to the ultimate community of the state, or to use Polyani's (2001) term, 're-instituted'. This is especially in the context of both an ideological as well as policy-practical attack on an interventionist-state spearheaded by neo-liberalism, and a simple-minded Marxist critique calling for its abolition.

It is in relation to supporting the left hand of the state, the state conceived in a qualified Hegelian and Durkheimian sense, as a state idea, protecting the universal or general interest of the population and offering it security, solidarity and equality in the face of increasing neo-liberalism on the one hand, and Marxist views that the state can be abolished on the other, that Bourdieu develops his theory of the state in *On The State*. Neo-liberalism has led, he argues elsewhere, 'to the withering away of the Hegelian-Durkheimian view of the state as a collective authority with a responsibility to act as the collective will and consciousness, and duty to make decisions in keeping with the general interest and contribute to promoting greater solidarity'.[82] The reference to 'withering away' may be an intended reference to French Marxists who had also called for the abolition of the state, a view that paradoxically chimes with neo-liberalism.[83] In this sense, Bourdieu is criticising Marxists from a Durkheimian-Hegelian socio-political standpoint though it remains unclear whether this is French Marxists extant in the French intellectual field at the time, or Marxism generally, or both. What is clear is that the polemical nature of his attack on Marxist approaches entails not only a simplified view of Marx's – rather than Marxists – view of the state and its abolition, which was not only more complex but as we noted in the third chapter, changing and developing throughout his work.[84] It also remains unclear to what extent Bourdieu accepts Durkheim and Hegel's overall view of the state.

---

[82] Bourdieu, *Social Structures*, p. 11.

[83] I owe this insight to Jeremy Lane – personal communication.

[84] Corrigan and Sayer Revolution Against the state: The Context & Significance of Marx's Later Writings, *Dialectical Anthropology* 12: 65–82. 1987. Jessop, *The Capitalist State*.

Both theories of the state also express ideological rationalisations of extant political processes, they constitute political acts: Hegel expressing the ideas of the Prussian reform movement led by Humboldt and Hardenberg; and Durkheim the arguments and concerns of the Republican elite in France as outlined in the philosophy of *solidarisme* which more or less stood as the doctrine of the Third Republic. Given the intrinsic co-constitutive relationship between state formation and individualisation, the latter process necessitates the mediating role of corporations existing between the individual and state to prevent the emergence of authoratarianism, and a dislocation between the two spheres. Such mediating institutions, however, remain absent in Bourdieu's account. Moreover, although they share similar visions in which rational and moral autonomy based on science or reason ultimately defeats self-interest, there are also stark differences between Hegel and Durkheim. The former, as we noted above, argued for a state based on constitutional monarchy in which the working classes were excluded – unable to enter into the state via the *Korporations* or as members of estates, *Stande*. To that extent Bourdieu's analysis appears closer to Durkheim's more classical Republican position, though Durkheim's focus on the moral recomposition of society based on solidarity rather than class-based politics, partly distances Bourdieu from a wholesale alignment with that political standpoint.

With the emergence and growing recognition of the importance of the cultural or symbolic dimension of the state, there has been a corresponding shift away from earlier interpretations foregrounding force and violence or socio-material processes as benchmark attributes of the state. As Morgan and Orloff rightly note, however: 'states need to be conceptualised as *interlinked* or mutually constitutive forms of material and cultural power'.[85] One can, therefore, use Bourdieu to criticize *certain* Marxist theories of the state for their lack of acknowledgement of non-economic and particularly socio-cultural processes and their failure to see – though Marx himself did in fact see – the progressive as well as regressive aspect of the state.[86] This criticism equally applies to the Hintzian or neo-Weberian

[85] Morgan and Orloff, p. 19.
[86] See for example, Marx, Karl, *The Communist Manifesto*.

theories of the state foregounding force and violence. But at the same time, one can also use Weberian or bellicist approaches against Bourdieu for his failure to acknowledge the importance of physical force. Similarly Marxism can be employed to criticize some of the weaknesses in Bourdieu's under-emphasis of the importance of social relations of production, exploitation and over-emphasis of cultural processes as the basis for social domination. As we noted earlier Marx, in his critique of the Hegelian state and later, recognised that the state itself was conditioned by the economy and rather than being able to control it, inescapably expressed the contradictions within it, albeit in a mediated form. As he notes 'civil society must assert itself in its external relations as nationality and internally must organise itself as State.'[87] It was for this reason that he argued that the capitalist state had to be abolished.

By endorsing this alternative Marxist view, my intention is not simply to highlight an enduring tension between the Republican and a Marxist explanatory framework, or between right and left Hegelians, again producing another unhelpful binary that either emphasizes politics or the economy in the understanding of the state and bringing us back to well-trodden debates between state-centred and neo-Marxist accounts of the state. Rather, since both processes are integral, and the separation between the economic and political aspect of social formations is in fact itself a historical outcome, it is a question of the balance between these two concepts and processes in explaining empirical manifestations of state power and actions, acknowledging both the reality of the state and the state of economic reality.

The Continuing Relevance of Bourdieu?

Having made these criticism, I will now make what appears to be a *volta face*. Without doubt in terms of explanatory ambition and empirical detail Bourdieu's sociological framework has made one of the most important and lasting contributions to sociology. But there are more problems characterising his theory of the state than generally pertain to his sociological theory.

---

[87] Cited in Corrigan and Sayer, Revolution Against the State: The Contexty & Significance of Marx's Later Writings, *Dialectical Anthropology* 12. 1987, p. 73.

Although flawed, the weaker conception of the state and symbolic domination does still constitute a dynamic and creative corrective to standard views which often neglect the role of cultural forms and social classifications in maintaining and reproducing forms of power and domination. Bourdieu's concepts have been forged in the context of a rich stream of empirical studies. Their utility derives from their capacity consistently to generate insights underpinning substantive research programmes. His reflexive genetic approach, when married with other more 'materialist' approaches, still provides the basis for examining the development of state administrative systems centred on authority, the role of performatives, integration as a precondition of domination, and the self-referential nature of knowledge tied to state legitimation. The emphasis on the state's power of nomination, classification and official validation, in facilitating the construction of both groups and modes of identification, sanctioning and defining social practices, and the cleavages that exist within the state itself – of 'antagonistic co-operation' – are also all useful for understanding the modern state. In contrast to many highly abstract Marxist and Weberian accounts, what Bourdieu's theory provides is the basis of a concrete research programme, replete with macro, meso- and micro-level concepts.

Weber had long ago recognised the diversity in state functions when he noted that there were few activities that the state had not been involved in 'from the provision of subsistence to the patronage of the arts'.[88] More recently, Morgan and Orloff have talked about 'The many hands of the state'.[89] As it stands, and given its one-sidedness, Bourdieu's theory of the state needs to be utilised in instrumental terms: as productive in investigating certain empirical research contexts or problems dealing with the state, and more limited in others. For example, if we analyse the Irish state historically his approach has only a restricted validity in examining the violent inter-state conflicts that generated the formation of the State in Ireland, nor the capacious role of the Catholic Church in regulating morality and hence the religious dimension of the state. Yet, it retains a powerful explanatory value when examining the Irish state's response to the arrival of migrants, for instance. All States classify and assign migrants into specific

---

[88] Weber, Max, *Economy and Society: An Outline of Interpretive Sociology.* p. 58.
[89] Morgan and Orloff, The Many Hands of the State.

legal and political categories – or differentiated immigration statuses. In Ireland, as in other countries, state classifications were used as both regulatory and status devices in the treatment and management of immigrants arriving in Ireland. Some of these categories originated within an international legal context, others within the state, and still others in society generally. Processes of official classification conditioned the level of entry for all migrants as well as the variations within each of the immigrant status categories. These categories determine how migrants are seen by others and see themselves especially on the basis of a distinction between citizens and others. As Bourdieu's colleague Sayad (2004) notes, 'It is as though it were in the very nature of the state to discriminate ... to make the distinction, without which there can be no national state, between the "nationals" it recognizes as such and in which it therefore recognizes itself, just as they recognize themselves in it (this double mutual recognition effect is indispensable to the existence and function of the state), and "others" with whom it deals only in "material" or instrumental terms. It deals with them only because they are present within the field of its national sovereignty and in the national territory covered by that sovereignty'.[90] Rather than providing all residents with the same civil, political rights, social and economic rights state bureaucratic classification schemes discriminate and empower in different ways. The power of naming transmutes or reclassifies the person named, functioning almost as a rigid designator shaping his or her life chances, 'So that the fate of groups is bound up with the words that designate them.'[91] Through its unassailable vantage point, the Irish State assigns each group its place in the social order.

Nevertheless, state forms of classification and the treatment migrants received from the state were challenged, even by the most disempowered immigrant groups, including asylum seekers themselves. The protests held by asylum seekers in Direct Provision centres between 2012 and 2014 demonstrate this, though their role in challenging the continued existence of the Direct Provision system generally should not be overstated.

Bourdieu's theory of the state yields two different interpretations, oscillating between a view of an omnipotent strong invasive state, the fount and origin of classifications, beliefs, morals and values – the state

[90] A. Sayad, *The Suffering of the Immigrantnt*, Cambridge: Polity. 2004, p. 279.
[91] Bourdieu, *Distinction*, p. 481.

as everything, and a weaker view of a delimited state as a contested outcome of social struggles within the state and between the state and various groups standing outside of it. It is a theory dependent on an polysemous notion of symbolic capital, and of providing an analysis that although claiming to have superseded other accounts of the state, fails to address a number of significant issues that these approaches deal with including the international context of state activity, war and violence, and social class. Finally, it has been suggested that Bourdieu's theory should be read simultaneously, but irreducibly, as a theoretical and a political intervention situated between the poles of neo-liberalism and Marxism – which helps to explain some of its characteristics and deficiencies.

Although his theory is not without problems, it nevertheless retains a certain validity especially with its focus on symbolic and cultural processes of state classification. In order to be used more effectively, these need to be integrally conjoined with a recognition of the importance of material processes entailing war, violence and class exploitation.